REWARDS Plus

Reading Excellence: Word Attack & Rate Development Strategies

Reading Strategies
~ Applied to ~
Social Studies Passages

Anita L. Archer, Ph.D.

Mary M. Gleason, Ph.D.

Vicky Vachon, Ph.D.

Assisted by Beth Cooper

SOPRIS WEST™ EDUCATIONAL SERVICES
A CAMBIUM LEARNING COMPANY

BOSTON, MA • LONGMONT, CO

ISBN 13 Digit: 978-1-57035-803-6
ISBN 10 Digit: 1-57035-803-6
24037/3-12

Printed in the United States of America
Published and Distributed by

Sopris West™
EDUCATIONAL SERVICES

A Cambium Learning Company

4093 Specialty Place • Longmont, Colorado 80504
(303) 651-2829 • www.sopriswest.com

Cover photograph of Great Wall of China ©R. Ian Lloyd, Masterfile
Cover photograph of ship ©Doug Logan, Istockphoto
Cover photograph of Earth from space ©Bill Brooks, Masterfile
Cover photographs of Gandhi and immigrants ©2003 www.clipart.com

CONTENTS

ACTIVITY A *Vowel Combinations*

ay	ai	au
(say)	(rain)	(sauce)

er	ir	ur	ar
(her)	(bird)	(turn)	(farm)

ACTIVITY B *Vowel Conversions*

a   i   o

ACTIVITY C *Prefixes and Suffixes*

discover	dis	advertise	ad
mistaken	mis	insert	in
abdomen	ab	immediate	im

(ACTIVITY D) *Strategy Instruction*

1. abstract	insist	impact
2. distraught	misfit	admit

(ACTIVITY E) *Strategy Practice*

1. birthday	misplay	discard
2. maintain	disband	indistinct
3. modern	addict	imprint
4. absurd	insert	railway

(ACTIVITY F) *Sentence Reading*

1. If you have a ticket, they will admit you to the theater.
2. You maintain a machine by taking care of it.
3. My mother hopes to discard all her old clothes.
4. The play's plot was absurd, so the actors must disband.
5. The markings on the bird were indistinct.
6. My sister must learn to not be a misfit.
7. Marcos will insist on buying a new car this year.
8. His abstract paintings had an impact.
9. My bad day left me feeling distraught.
10. Jasmine left an imprint of her hand in the sand.

ACTIVITY A *Vowel Combinations*

a—e	o—e	i—e	e—e	u—e
(make)	(hope)	(side)	(Pete)	(use)

1.	er	ir	au	ai	a—e
2.	ar	u—e	ay	i—e	au
3.	e—e	ir	ai	o—e	u—e
4.	ur	ay	a—e	au	i—e

ACTIVITY B *Vowel Conversions*

a   i   o   u

ACTIVITY C *Prefixes and Suffixes*

compare	com	prevent	pre
belong	be	protect	pro
return	re	depart	de

1.	pro	be	pre	ad	dis	mis
2.	com	in	im	re	ab	de

(ACTIVITY D) *Strategy Instruction*

1.	beside	readjust	prepay
2.	combine	provide	defraud

(ACTIVITY E) *Strategy Practice*

1.	backbone	reprint	costume
2.	mistake	promote	prescribe
3.	obsolete	propose	sunstroke
4.	decode	holiday	subscribe

(ACTIVITY F) *Sentence Reading*

1. On my holiday, I will go by railway.
2. If you do a really good job, we will promote you.
3. Dr. Smith will readjust your backbone.
4. Dr. Smith will prescribe pills and provide a splint.
5. Dr. Smith will also help you with sunstroke.
6. It is a mistake to defraud people of their money.
7. Can you decode all the words in the reprint?
8. Do you subscribe to *USA TODAY*?
9. You will need to prepay for the holiday trip.
10. What costume do you propose to wear?

ACTIVITY A *Vowel Combinations*

	oi (void)	oy (boy)	or (torn)	
	ee (deep)	oa (foam)	ou (loud)	
1. er	a—e	oi	oy	ee
2. u—e	ou	au	or	oa
3. e—e	ir	ai	i—e	ar
4. o—e	ur	ay	au	ou

ACTIVITY B *Vowel Conversions*

a   i   o   u   e

ACTIVITY C *Prefixes and Suffixes*

continue	con	above	a
permit	per	example	ex
uncover	un	entail	en

1. per	con	dis	a	pre	de
2. com	pro	en	ab	im	mis
3. ex	con	un	com	a	pre

(ACTIVITY D) *Strategy Practice*

1. perturb	uncurl	confess
2. afraid	expert	engrave

(ACTIVITY E) *Independent Strategy Practice*

1. misinform	disagree	spellbound
2. sweepstake	reproduce	protect
3. turmoil	bemoan	discontent
4. imperfect	boycott	reconstruct

(ACTIVITY F) *Sentence Reading*

1. Mr. Lin was discontent even after winning the sweepstakes.

2. I confess that the mistake will perturb me.

3. Can you reproduce the reprint?

4. We will reconstruct the house this summer.

5. Can you provide an expert who will not misinform us?

6. You should protect yourself from sunstroke.

7. Sometimes you disagree even with an expert.

8. The addict has an imperfect life.

9. The chance to win the sweepstakes held him spellbound.

10. Don't be afraid to decode words like **reconstruct** and **discontent.**

ACTIVITY A *Vowel Combinations*

ow

(low)   (down)

1. ou	ow	i—e	oy	ur
2. oa	a—e	ow	ai	ir
3. oi	ow	ee	ow	ar
4. au	or	oy	u—e	ow

ACTIVITY B *Vowel Conversions*

u   e   i   a   o

ACTIVITY C *Prefixes and Suffixes*

birds	s	frantic	ic
running	ing	regulate	ate
landed	ed	selfish	ish
		artist	ist
kindness	ness	realism	ism
useless	less	biggest	est
final	al	tailor	or
careful	ful	farmer	er

1. ab	com	con	dis	pre	re
2. im	ex	un	per	pro	a
3. est	ic	ful	or	al	er
4. ish	ism	less	ate	ness	ist

(**ACTIVITY D**) *Strategy Practice*

1. regardless	softness	unfortunate
2. programmer	slowest	historical
3. organism	inventor	personal

(**ACTIVITY E**) *Independent Strategy Practice*

1. abnormal	respectful	proposal
2. exaggerate	exhaust	untruthful
3. careless	unfaithful	astonish
4. alarmist	energetic	exclude

(**ACTIVITY F**) *Sentence Reading*

1. The programmer was exhausted from all the turmoil.
2. Everyone is respectful to the well-known inventor.
3. It is unfortunate that the respected inventor's proposal will not work.
4. It is a historical fact that some experts exaggerate.
5. Samuel's personal proposal was astonishing.
6. Regardless of the fact that some experts are untruthful and unfaithful, most would not defraud.
7. Because of her abnormal backbone, Vanessa must not be careless or too energetic.
8. Jason was discontent and bemoaned his job on the railway.
9. The tricks will astonish you and leave you spellbound.
10. We should not exclude anyone from winning the sweepstakes.

ACTIVITY A Vowel Combinations

oo

(moon)   (book)

1. ow	oa	oi	oo	oy
2. ee	ou	er	ir	au
3. ay	oo	a—e	ur	oo
4. ar	ai	ow	oo	au

ACTIVITY B Vowel Conversions

e   i   a   u   o

ACTIVITY C Prefixes and Suffixes

ac**tion**	tion	milit**ary**	ary
mis**sion**	sion	odd**ity**	ity
mill**ion**	ion	dorm**ant**	ant
atten**tive**	tive	disturb**ance**	ance
expen**sive**	sive	consist**ent**	ent
industr**y**	y	ess**ence**	ence
safe**ly**	ly	argu**ment**	ment

1. al	con	a	com	er
2. tion	or	ly	sive	ance
3. tive	ary	ence	ent	ant
4. ity	ment	y	ion	est
5. ful	ity	sion	ance	ant

(ACTIVITY D) *Strategy Practice*

1. advertisement   delightful   disinfectant
2. intentionally   property   expressionless
3. personality   admittance   incoherence

(ACTIVITY E) *Independent Strategy Practice*

1. perfectionist   independently   dictionary
2. contaminate   precautionary   deductive
3. inconsistently   excitement   repulsive
4. opinion   hoodwink   imperfect

(ACTIVITY F) *Sentence Reading*

1. The imperfect dictionary had many mistakes.
2. An advertisement should not intentionally misinform people.
3. A perfectionist will be discontent in a job with people who are unfaithful and disrespectful.
4. As a precautionary step, we should not contaminate our water.
5. Your classmates might disagree with your opinion.
6. We were delighted by the excitement of the energetic teacher.
7. Peter independently made a proposal for admittance to the club.
8. Unfortunately, the art was inconsistently reproduced when reprinted.
9. The energetic team members had delightful personalities.
10. Her statements were untruthful and disrespectful.

ACTIVITY A · *Vowel Combinations*

ea
(meat)   (thread)

1. oo	ea	ow	ee	er	ai
2. au	ay	e—e	oy	ea	ur
3. oa	i—e	ir	ea	ar	oi
4. ow	ur	ea	oo	oi	au

ACTIVITY B · *Vowel Conversions*

u   i   a   e   o

ACTIVITY C · *Prefixes and Suffixes*

nerv**ous**	ous	cour**age**	age
pre**cious**	cious	pic**ture**	ture
cau**tious**	tious	dispos**able**	able
spe**cial**	cial	revers**ible**	ible
par**tial**	tial	crad**le**	le

1. per	a	con	com	ex
2. ous	able	ment	le	ent
3. al	age	ture	cious	tial
4. ion	ible	y	ance	or
5. ity	cial	ence	ant	tious

(ACTIVITY D) *Strategy Practice*

1. official	substantial	delicious
2. pretentious	impressionable	incombustible
3. conjecture	inconspicuous	disadvantage

(ACTIVITY E) *Independent Strategy Practice*

1. administrative	performance	threadbare
2. circumstantial	investigation	professionalism
3. precipitation	environmentally	communication
4. unconventional	consolidate	misconception

(ACTIVITY F) *Sentence Reading*

1. In an attempt to reduce the size of the federal government, administrative departments will be consolidated.
2. Devon did not find his companion's sarcastic comments entertaining.
3. The written communication contained a number of misconceptions.
4. The children watching the evening performance were inconspicuous.
5. Consistency and professionalism are qualities needed in all occupations.
6. The defendant could not submit the circumstantial evidence from the investigation.
7. All corporations thrive on effective organization and environmentally safe conditions.
8. Historically, our population has always been environmentally concerned.
9. Most impressionable children do not act independently.
10. While the instructor's methods were unconventional, the results were tremendous.

(ACTIVITY A) *Vocabulary*

List 1: Tell

1.	Thrace	*n.* ▶	(a region of Greece)
2.	Thracians	*n.* ▶	(the people of Thrace)
3.	Dionysus	*n.* ▶	(a Greek god)
4.	Thespis	*n.* ▶	(a Greek actor)
5.	Pisistratus	*n.* ▶	(a ruler of ancient Greece)
6.	chorus	*n.* ▶	(a group of singers)
7.	dithyramb	*n.* ▶	(a chant)
8.	dialogue	*n.* ▶	(a conversation in a play)
9.	ceremony	*n.* ▶	(activities done on an important occasion)
10.	theatrical	*adj.* ▶	(relating to the theater)

List 2: Strategy Practice

1.	production	*n.* ▶	(a play, movie, or video)
2.	protagonist	*n.* ▶	(the main character in a play)
3.	audience	*n.* ▶	(a group of people gathered to see a production)
4.	commentary	*n.* ▶	(a series of comments or explanations)
5.	morality	*n.* ▶	(whether an act is right or wrong)
6.	tradition	*n.* ▶	(doing something the same way it was done in the past)
7.	visible	*adj.* ▶	(can be seen)
8.	accommodate	*v.* ▶	(to make room for)
9.	appreciate	*v.* ▶	(to like something)
10.	interact	*v.* ▶	(to talk with someone)

TALLY ☐   VOCABULARY

Points

List 3: Word Families

Family 1	religion	*n.* ▶	(a set of beliefs or moral principles)
	religious	*adj.*	
	religiously	*adv.*	
Family 2	compete	*v.* ▶	(to strive against others; to try to win)
	competition	*n.*	
	competitive	*adj.*	
Family 3	politics	*n.* ▶	(activities related to the government)
	political	*adj.*	
	politically	*adv.*	
Family 4	tragedy	*n.* ▶	(a play with a sad ending)
	tragic	*adj.*	
	tragically	*adv.*	
Family 5	comedy	*n.* ▶	(a play that is funny)
	comedic	*adj.*	
	comedian	*n.*	

(ACTIVITY B) *Spelling Dictation*

1.	**4.**
2.	**5.**
3.	**6.**

SPELLING ⬛ **6**

Points

(ACTIVITY C) *Background Knowledge*

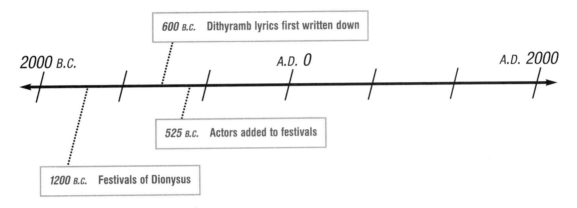

Many things that we experience today began thousands of years ago in another country. This article tells us about the development of theater in ancient Greece between 1200 B.C. and 525 B.C. During that period of time, the Greek civilization thrived around the Mediterranean Sea. The Greek people produced amazing cultural accomplishments in art and literature that continue to influence us today.

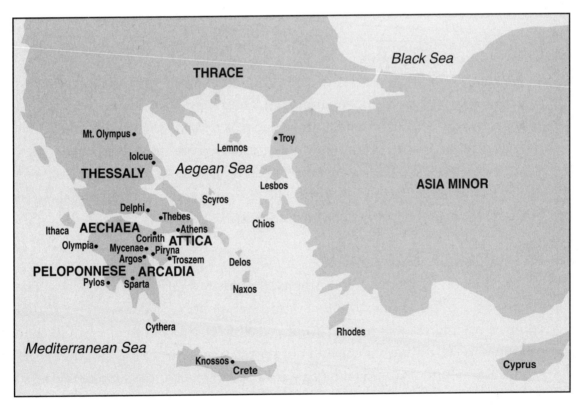

Map of Ancient Greece

(ACTIVITY D) *Passage Reading and Comprehension*

Greek Theater

When you think of theater, you might imagine a play performed at your
13 | school, an evening at the opera, or even a Broadway musical. But theater was
27 | born 2500 years ago in Greece. Theater began there as a religious ceremony. (#1)

40 | **The Cult of Dionysus**
44 | Around 1200 B.C., in northern Greece, there was a region known as Thrace.
57 | In spring festivals and rituals, the Thracians worshipped Dionysus, the Greek
68 | god of fertility. The worshippers used dancing, feasting, storytelling, and animal
79 | sacrifice to tell the god's stories and legends. When the beliefs in Dionysus
92 | began to spread southward to different tribes in Greece, the ceremonies became
104 | more formal and symbolic. By 600 B.C., these rituals were part of spring
117 | festivities throughout Greece. The storytellers wore masks and chanted their
127 | stories in choruses. The choruses did not sing like ours do today. They used a
142 | rhythmic, chanting form of speech known as the *dithyramb.* (#2)

151 | **Rituals Become Theater**
154 | In about 600 B.C., the lyrics to the dithyrambs were written down for the first
169 | time. About 75 years later, a man named Thespis added an actor who interacted
183 | with the chorus. Now the actor (also known as a *thespian*) would interact with
197 | the chorus, taking turns chanting the lyrics. When Thespis added a second actor,
210 | theater was born. Now the two actors related directly to each other, using
223 | dialogue and action to tell the story. The chorus added commentary and insight
236 | to what was occurring between the actors. (#3)

243 | **Drama Competitions**
245 | In 534 B.C., Pisistratus ruled Athens, the greatest city-state in Greece. He
258 | changed the Dionysian festival to a drama competition. This became a highly
270 | competitive and popular annual event. Wealthy people in the city would fund
282 | productions. In return, they would not have to pay taxes to the city that year. The
298 | drama competitions would take place over several whole days in the spring. (#4)

310 | **Amphitheaters**
311 | Athens, as well as other major Greek cities, built large theaters to
323 | accommodate this increasingly popular pastime. The amphitheaters were built

332	into hillsides, so that people sat on tiered seats, looking downward at the stage.
346	The stage was a raised platform, which helped make the actors visible. Between
359	the raised stage and the audience was the orchestra, a platform on which the
373	chorus was positioned. (#5)

Tragedy

376	
377	As theater became more and more popular, its forms began to change.
389	Between 600 and 500 B.C., the dithyramb evolved into the tragic play. Tragedies
402	were written as a sort of morality play, which shows the right and wrong paths in
418	life. In a tragedy, the main character (also known as the *protagonist*) is faced
432	with difficult decisions, circumstances, or obstacles. The protagonist suffers
441	throughout the story. This theatrical form enabled the playwrights to teach
452	lessons to the audience about how to live properly, how to respect the gods, and
467	how to behave in society. (#6)

Comedy

472	
473	Comedic plays also became popular with theatrical audiences. The comedies
483	focused on the humor in society. The people in Athens and other Greek cities
497	especially appreciated the use of satire. Satirical plays poked fun at common
509	aspects of city life, including culture, religion, and politics. Many of the comedic
522	stories the Greeks used are still used today. (#7)

Epilogue

530	
531	Although many Greek plays and theatrical traditions survive today, theater in
542	ancient Greece began to decline around 400 B.C., after the deaths of some of the
557	greatest playwrights. Shortly thereafter, Greece went to war with neighboring
567	states, eventually falling to Alexander the Great and his armies. But the forms
580	and practices of Greek theater spread into other cultures. Because of Greek
592	theater, we enjoy many kinds of theater today. (#8)
600	

(ACTIVITY E) Fluency Building

| Cold Timing | | Practice 1 | |
| Practice 2 | | Hot Timing | |

(ACTIVITY F) *Comprehension Questions—Multiple Choice*

Comprehension Strategy—Multiple Choice

Step 1: Read the item.

Step 2: Read all of the choices.

Step 3: Think about why each choice might be correct or incorrect. Check the article as needed.

Step 4: From the possible correct choices, select the best answer.

1. (Vocabulary) **What words from the article are synonyms?**
  a. **comedy** and **tragedy**
  b. **actor** and **thespian**
  c. **drama competition** and **production**
  d. a **play** and an **opera**

2. (Main Idea) **Theater was born when:**
  a. amphitheaters were built.
  b. choruses chanted dithyrambs.
  c. actors interacted with each other and the chorus.
  d. Pisistratus started drama competitions.

3. (Compare and Contrast) **What were the major differences between the stories told at the early spring festivals and the stories told by Thespis?**
  a. The early spring festival stories were told on grass fields, while Thespis's stories were told in amphitheaters.
  b. The early spring festivals occurred in northern Greece, while Thespis's stories were told in the southern part of Greece.
  c. The storytellers at the early spring festivals wore masks and chanted, and Thespis had the chorus wear costumes when they performed.
  d. In the early spring festivals, the choruses chanted a form of speech known as a *dithyramb*, but under Thespis, actors took turns chanting lyrics with the chorus.

4. (Cause and Effect) **What was the main reason that the amphitheaters were built?**
  a. Large amphitheaters allowed rulers to compete against other rulers from large cities in many activities, including sports.
  b. As the popularity of theater grew, amphitheaters allowed more people to enjoy productions.
  c. Amphitheaters were built as a way for wealthy people to avoid paying taxes.
  d. Amphitheaters were built so that people would need to look down to see the stage.

MULTIPLE CHOICE COMPREHENSION

4

Points

(ACTIVITY G) *Expository Writing—Summary*

Writing Strategy—Summary

Step 1: LIST (List the details that are important enough to include in the summary.)
Step 2: CROSS OUT (Reread the details. Cross out any that you decide not to include.)
Step 3: CONNECT (Connect any details that could go into one sentence.)
Step 4: NUMBER (Number the details in a logical order.)
Step 5: WRITE (Write your summary.)
Step 6: EDIT (Revise and proofread your summary.)

Prompt: Write a summary of the information you read in the *Greek Theater* article.

Example Summary Plan

Planning Box
(topic) *Greek Theater*
(detail) – *began as a religious ceremony*
(detail) – *honored the Greek god Dionysus*
(detail) – *beliefs in Dionysus began to spread southward*
(detail) – *choruses chanted lyrics*
(detail) – *actors joined the choruses*
(detail) – *the Dionysus festival in Athens became a drama competition*
(detail) – *amphitheaters were built*
(detail) – *performed tragedies that taught lessons*
(detail) – *performed comedies that made fun of life*
(detail) – *declined when playwrights died and the government changed*

Directions: Write your summary on a separate piece of paper.

Example Summary

The roots of modern theater can be found in early Greek theater. Greek theater began as a religious ceremony that honored the Greek god Dionysus. At first, choruses chanted lyrics. When actors were added to interact with the chorus, theater was born. Later, the Dionysus festival in Athens became a drama competition, and amphitheaters were built to accommodate the event. Both tragedies, which taught lessons, and comedies, which made fun of life, were performed. Greek theater declined when the great playwrights died and the government changed.

Rubric— Summary	Student or Partner Rating		Teacher Rating	
1. Did the author state the topic and the main idea in the first sentence?	Yes	Fix up	Yes	No
2. Did the author focus on important details?	Yes	Fix up	Yes	No
3. Did the author combine details in some of the sentences?	Yes	Fix up	Yes	No
4. Is the summary easy to understand?	Yes	Fix up	Yes	No
5. Did the author correctly spell words, particularly the words found in the article?	Yes	Fix up	Yes	No
6. Did the author use correct capitalization, capitalizing the first word in the sentence and proper names of people, places, and things?	Yes	Fix up	Yes	No
7. Did the author use correct punctuation, including a period at the end of each sentence?	Yes	Fix up	Yes	No

WRITING 7

Points

(ACTIVITY A) *Vocabulary*

List 1: Tell

1. **Marco Polo**   *n.*   ▶ (a 13th century traveler and storyteller)
2. **Italy**   *n.*   ▶ (a country in Europe)
3. **Venice**   *n.*   ▶ (a city in Italy)
4. **Venetian**   *adj.*   ▶ (pertaining to Venice or its people)
5. **Genoa**   *n.*   ▶ (a city in Italy)
6. **Genoese**   *adj.*   ▶ (pertaining to Genoa or its people)
7. **Mongolian**   *adj.*   ▶ (pertaining to Mongolia or its people)
8. **khan**   *n.*   ▶ (a ruler of ancient China)
9. **Rustichello**   *n.*   ▶ (a famous writer)
10. **porcelain**   *n.*   ▶ (a fine, white ceramic material)

List 2: Strategy Practice

1. **merchant**   *n.*   ▶ (a person whose job is buying and selling things)
2. **navigator**   *n.*   ▶ (a person who directs the course of a ship)
3. **voyage**   *n.*   ▶ (a trip, usually by ship)
4. **translate**   *v.*   ▶ (to change into another language)
5. **accompany**   *v.*   ▶ (to go along with)
6. **encourage**   *v.*   ▶ (to inspire)
7. **skepticism**   *n.*   ▶ (doubt or unbelief)
8. **diplomatic**   *adj.*   ▶ (pertaining to relationships between nations)
9. **relatively**   *adv.*   ▶ (somewhat)
10. **extensively**   *adv.*   ▶ (large in amount)

TALLY ☐   **VOCABULARY** ◹ 5

Points

List 3: Word Families

Family 1	**establish**	_v._	▶ (to set up permanently)
	established	_adj._	
	establishment	_n._	

Family 2	**converse**	_v._	▶ (to talk together)
	conversation	_n._	
	conversational	_adj._	

Family 3	**describe**	_v._	▶ (to tell about)
	description	_n._	
	descriptively	_adv._	

Family 4	**respect**	_v._	▶ (admiration of someone or something)
	respectful	_adj._	
	respectfully	_adv._	

Family 5	**inform**	_v._	▶ (to tell)
	information	_n._	
	informant	_n._	

ACTIVITY B _Spelling Dictation_

1.		**4.**	
2.		**5.**	
3.		**6.**	

SPELLING 6

Points

(ACTIVITY C) *Background Knowledge*

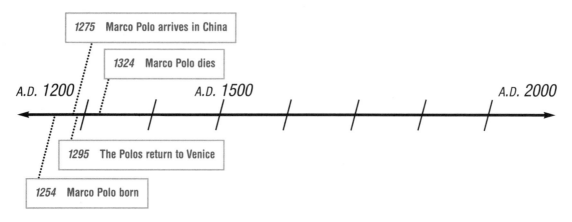

Since 100 B.C., a network of overland trade routes was developed to carry goods between Europe and Asia. These trade routes were called the "Silk Road" because of the valuable Chinese cloth that was transported on them. Trade continued on the Silk Road until ocean routes surpassed land routes in the 15th and 16th centuries A.D.

In this article, you will meet Marco Polo, who traveled with his father to China via the Silk Road. It is through his storytelling that we have learned a great deal about ancient China.

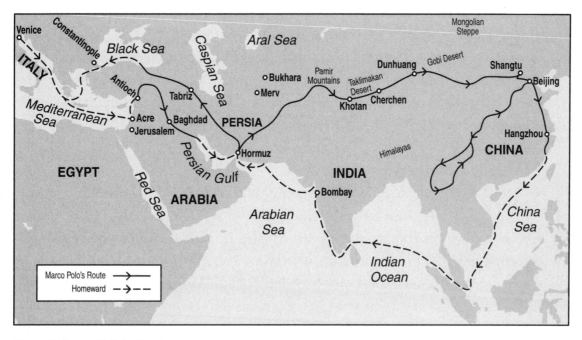

Map of Marco Polo's Route

(ACTIVITY D) *Passage Reading and Comprehension*

Marco Polo

	Born in Italy in the middle of the 13th century, Marco Polo was part of a
16	wealthy merchant family. His father and uncle had already been trading
27	extensively with Middle Eastern countries. They traded silk, porcelain, and
37	other exotic goods over the Silk Road. The Silk Road was a trading route
51	established between China and Rome. As a result, the Polos traveled a great
64	deal. Marco did not meet his father until he was 15 or 16, when his father
80	returned to Venice after many years of travel. This time, when he left again, he
95	took young Marco with him. (#1)

100	**Voyages to China**
103	The travelers set out overland rather than risk the sea route. They traveled
116	through what are now Armenia and Iran, through central Asia, across the
128	mountains, and across the Gobi Desert. In 1275, they arrived at the summer
141	court of Kublai Khan, near present-day Beijing, China. The khan, the ruler of
155	the area, warmly welcomed them, and he hired the Polos into his service. (#2)
168	Marco and his family spent the next 17 years working for Kublai Khan in
182	China. The khan had a special fondness for Marco's storytelling and
193	conversation. Marco was sent on diplomatic missions all over the empire. Each
205	time he returned to the khan, Marco had new stories and descriptions of the
219	lands and people he had seen. He was a highly respected diplomat and may
233	even have held a governing post in the city of Yangzhou. (#3)

244	**A Wish to Return Home**
249	The Polos made several requests to the khan that they should be allowed to
263	return to Europe. But they were denied these requests because Kublai Khan
275	was so fond of his Italian visitors. But finally, in 1292, he allowed them to
290	accompany a Mongolian princess who would be traveling to Persia by sea. Once
303	she had arrived safely, the Polos traveled back to Venice. They returned home in
317	1295. People flocked to hear Marco Polo's accounts of his travels, and they
330	called him *il milione*—the man with a million stories. (#4)

340	**A Fortunate Meeting**
343	Soon after his return to Venice, Marco got involved in the Venetian navy. He
357	was taken prisoner by the Genoese during a battle in the Mediterranean Sea.

370	He was sent to a prison in Genoa. In prison, he met Rustichello, a relatively
385	famous writer of romances and tales of chivalry. Rustichello was enchanted with
397	Marco Polo's tales of his travels in the Far East and agreed to write down the
413	stories. When the book was published, it became extremely popular and was
425	translated into several languages. (#5)
429	Marco Polo was released from prison and returned to Venice. He died there
442	in 1324. But his book continued to tell his stories of travels in China. It became
458	a sort of handbook for merchants and navigators. Christopher Columbus had a
470	copy that was printed in Latin, which he often referred to while planning his
484	western route to Eastern countries. (#6)
489	**Skepticism**
490	As popularity of Marco Polo's book grew, so did questions about its
502	truthfulness. Maybe people felt that the stories were simply too fabulous to be
515	believed. But Marco maintained that they were true right up until his death. On
529	his deathbed, when encouraged to retract the "fables" he had spread, Marco
541	replied by saying that he had not told half of what he had seen—he was afraid it
559	would not be believed. Since his death, scholars have been able to verify much
573	of the information that Marco Polo collected, earning him a place as one of the
588	greatest travelers in the world. (#7)
593	

(ACTIVITY E) *Fluency Building*

Cold Timing		Practice 1	

Practice 2		Hot Timing	

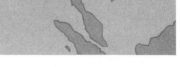

(ACTIVITY F) *Comprehension Questions—Multiple Choice*

Comprehension Strategy—Multiple Choice

Step 1: Read the item.
Step 2: Read all of the choices.
Step 3: Think about why each choice might be correct or incorrect. Check the article as needed.
Step 4: From the possible correct choices, select the best answer.

1. (Vocabulary) **Read these sentences from the passage: "Marco was sent on diplomatic *missions* all over the empire. Each time he returned to the khan, Marco had new stories and descriptions of the lands and people he had seen." Based on the wording of those sentences, what does the word *missions* mean?**
   a. Places used by missionaries for religious work.
   b. Tasks that a person is sent to perform.
   c. Books containing stories of adventurers.
   d. A group of diplomats assigned to a foreign country.

2. (Main Idea) **If the article needed a new title, which would be best?**
   a. *The Traveler*
   b. *The Prisoner*
   c. *Father and Son*
   d. *The Diplomat*

3. (Cause and Effect) **Why was it beneficial for Marco to have met Rustichello in prison?**
   a. Rustichello enjoyed Marco's stories, which made Marco feel better.
   b. Rustichello joined Marco on his journeys to China.
   c. Rustichello used details from Marco's travels in his romances.
   d. Rustichello wrote down Marco's stories, which later became a book.

4. (Compare and Contrast) **What did Marco Polo and Rustichello have in common?**
   a. They both wrote books.
   b. They both were imprisoned.
   c. They both loved adventures
   d. They both enjoyed travel to China.

MULTIPLE CHOICE COMPREHENSION

4

(ACTIVITY G) *Expository Writing—Summary*

Writing Strategy—Summary

Step 1: LIST (List the details that are important enough to include in the summary.)
Step 2: CROSS OUT (Reread the details. Cross out any that you decide not to include.)
Step 3: CONNECT (Connect any details that could go into one sentence.)
Step 4: NUMBER (Number the details in a logical order.)
Step 5: WRITE (Write your summary.)
Step 6: EDIT (Revise and proofread your summary.)

Prompt: Write a summary of the information you read about Marco Polo.

Planning Box
(topic)
(detail)
(detail)
(detail)
(detail)
(detail)
(detail)
(detail)
(detail)
(detail)

Directions: Write your summary on a separate piece of paper.

Rubric—Summary	Student or Partner Rating	Teacher Rating
1. Did the author state the topic and the main idea in the first sentence?	Yes Fix up	Yes No
2. Did the author focus on important details?	Yes Fix up	Yes No
3. Did the author combine details in some of the sentences?	Yes Fix up	Yes No
4. Is the summary easy to understand?	Yes Fix up	Yes No
5. Did the author correctly spell words, particularly the words found in the article?	Yes Fix up	Yes No
6. Did the author use correct capitalization, capitalizing the first word in the sentence and proper names of people, places, and things?	Yes Fix up	Yes No
7. Did the author use correct punctuation, including a period at the end of each sentence?	Yes Fix up	Yes No

WRITING   7

Points

(ACTIVITY A) *Vocabulary*

List 1: Tell

1. **pirate**   *n.* ▶ (a person who robs on the high seas)
2. **privateer**   *n.* ▶ (a crew member of a privately owned ship who attacks enemies on behalf of a government)
3. **buccaneer**   *n.* ▶ (a pirate who attacked Spanish ships)
4. **circumnavigate**   *v.* ▶ (to sail completely around the earth)

List 2: Strategy Practice

1. **romanticize**   *v.* ▶ (to make romantic)
2. **plunder**   *v.* ▶ (to take things by force)
3. **jurisdiction**   *n.* ▶ (territory ruled by a government)
4. **intention**   *n.* ▶ (purpose)
5. **sponsorship**   *n.* ▶ (the act of assuming responsibility for a person or thing)
6. **nutrition**   *n.* ▶ (the process by which the body takes in and uses food)
7. **engagement**   *n.* ▶ (an encounter, conflict, or battle)
8. **international**   *adj.* ▶ (concerning two or more countries)
9. **regulation**   *n.* ▶ (a rule or law)
10. **intensity**   *n.* ▶ (strength)

TALLY ☐   VOCABULARY ◪ 5

Points

List 3: Word Families

Family 1	**inspire**	*v.*	▶ (to influence; to fill with courage)
	inspiration	*n.*	
	inspirational	*adj.*	

Family 2	**class**	*n.*	▶ (a grouping of things together that are alike)
	classify	*v.*	
	classification	*n.*	

Family 3	**theory**	*n.*	▶ (an idea that explains an event)
	theoretical	*adj.*	
	theoretically	*adv.*	

Family 4	**adventure**	*n.*	▶ (a thrilling or exciting experience)
	adventurous	*adj.*	
	adventuresome	*adj.*	

Family 5	**democracy**	*n.*	▶ (a government run by the people)
	democratic	*adj.*	
	democratically	*adv.*	

(ACTIVITY B) *Spelling Dictation*

1.		**4.**	
2.		**5.**	
3.		**6.**	

SPELLING 6

Points

ACTIVITY C) *Background Knowledge*

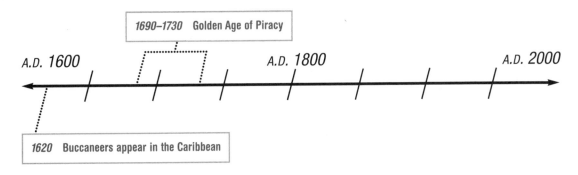

1690–1730 Golden Age of Piracy

A.D. *1600*   A.D. *1800*   A.D. *2000*

1620 Buccaneers appear in the Caribbean

In this article, you will be reading about the Golden Age of Piracy in the 17th and 18th centuries. During this time, many ships sailed from Europe to the New World (North and South America) to obtain land and resources, such as gold. When the ships returned to Europe, they were often laden with valuable cargo, including gold. Pirates desiring these goods had little difficulty attacking the merchant ships because the navies of Spain and England had little presence in the seas off the coast of Florida, in the Caribbean, and off the shores of South America. Because of conflicts between Spain and England, some acts of piracy were supported even by the governments.

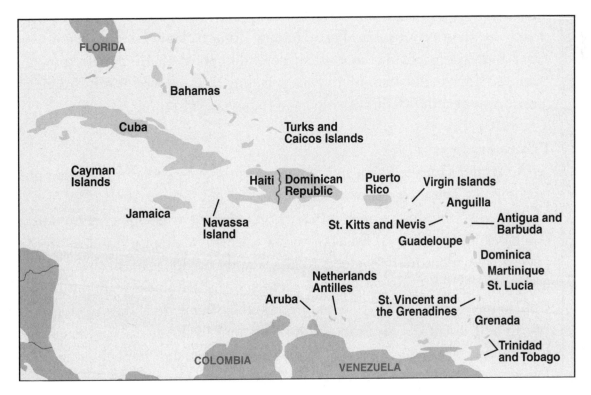

Map of the Caribbean

ACTIVITY D *Passage Reading and Comprehension*

Pirates and Piracy

What Are Pirates?

3	Pirates are familiar characters. Books and movies like *Peter Pan* or *Treasure*
15	*Island* have romanticized them. But real pirates are criminals, known especially
26	for attacking ships and stealing their cargo while on the high seas. Piracy is
40	different from other types of robbery because it occurs outside the jurisdiction
52	of any one government. Although pirates existed in Roman times and still do
65	today, the ones who inspired the famous images in the movies lived in the 17th
80	and 18th centuries. This era is known as the "Golden Age of Piracy." (#1)
93	Several different kinds of pirates sailed the seas, stealing goods from other
105	ships. Because they came from various countries and differed in their intentions,
117	they were called pirates, privateers, buccaneers, or marooners. (#2)

125	**Pirates**
126	The term *pirates* refers to a general classification of sailors who used their
139	skills to attack other ships. The pirates attacked any ship that seemed to have
153	something worth stealing, whether it was gold, precious cargo, or the ship itself.
166	Unlike other types of pirates, these sailors plundered ships from all nations
178	strictly for their private gain. Bartholomew Roberts, known more commonly as
189	Black Bart, was probably the most successful pirate ever. He captured more
201	than 400 ships in less than four years, traveling the coasts of South America,
215	North America, the Caribbean, and the Bahamas. (#3)

222	**Privateers**
223	A privateer traveled on a ship that carried official papers from a government
236	or company. These papers were called a *Letter of Marque*. The Letter of
249	Marque gave the ship permission to act on behalf of a specific government or
263	company. For example, if England was at war with Spain, the English
275	government sponsored privateers to attack and plunder Spanish ships.
284	Theoretically, the Letter of Marque protected the privateers from punishment.
294	But frequently they were tried and punished by the nations they were
306	"permitted" to attack. Sir Francis Drake, famous for being the first Englishman
318	to circumnavigate the globe, was a privateer for England. His ship attacked and
331	looted Spanish ships as he traveled in the name of Queen Elizabeth. (#4)

343	**Buccaneers**
344	Buccaneers were French, English, and Dutch pirates who specifically
353	targeted Spanish commerce ships in the Spanish Main (the coastal areas from
365	northern Florida through the Caribbean and along South America). These
375	pirates differed from privateers because they did not have any state sponsorship.
387	They manned smaller ships than did other pirates, focusing on inlets, bays, and
400	other shallow waters. (#5)
403	**Life on a Ship**
407	In the movies, the life of a pirate seems adventurous and exciting. In reality,
421	however, it was difficult and dangerous. The pirates did not eat well because
434	fresh food rotted quickly. They ate mostly hard tack (a dry, plain biscuit) and
448	dried meat, which didn't give them much nutrition. Water often went bad,
460	forcing the pirates to drink beer and rum instead. Many pirates got food
473	poisoning or seasickness. The ships had no toilets and smelled terribly. (#6)
484	Even though the captain was in charge, the ships were often run democratically.
497	The whole crew voted on an issue. Members of the crew obeyed rules, known as
512	*articles*. The articles included rules of conduct for the ship, punishments for crimes
525	committed, and rules of engagement with other ships. (#7)
533	**Pirates Today**
535	Piracy still occurs today in several different forms. People who steal
546	computer software are known as pirates. In the Caribbean and the South China
559	seas, armed men still board ships to take over the crew and cargo. Instead of
574	large sailing ships, they use small motorboats. Although criminals still sail on the
587	high seas, international law, trade regulations, and naval patrols ensure that
598	piracy will never again return to the intensity of its golden years. (#8)
610	

(ACTIVITY E) *Fluency Building*

Cold Timing			Practice 1		

Practice 2			Hot Timing		

(ACTIVITY F) *Comprehension Questions—Multiple Choice*

Comprehension Strategy—Multiple Choice

Step 1: Read the item.

Step 2: Read all of the choices.

Step 3: Think about why each choice might be correct or incorrect. Check the article as needed.

Step 4: From the possible correct choices, select the best answer.

1. (Vocabulary) **Read this sentence from the passage: "Piracy is different from other types of robbery because it occurs outside the *jurisdiction* of any one government." What does the word *jurisdiction* mean in that sentence?**

    a. The intention of a government.

    b. The territory governed by one country.

    c. Walled cities found within a country.

    d. The jury system of a country.

2. (Compare and Contrast) **What was the major difference between *pirates* and *privateers*?**

    a. Pirates were primarily from Spain, while privateers were from England.

    b. Pirates would attack any ship to steal items of value, but privateers focused their attacks on ships of enemy countries.

    c. The goal of the pirates was to steal items of value. However, the goal of privateers was to destroy other ships.

    d. Pirates were sailors by profession, while privateers were military commanders.

3. (Main Idea) **Which sentence gives the best summary of the article?**

    a. During the Golden Age of Piracy, there were a number of types of pirates, including pirates, privateers, and buccaneers.

    b. Pirates attacked ships to take gold.

    c. Life was very difficult for pirates because of the poor quality of their food and water.

    d. While the life of pirates has often been made very glamorous in movies, it was actually very difficult and dangerous.

4. (Cause and Effect) **Why were privateers often tried and punished by the nations they were "permitted" to attack?**

    a. The privateers did not always have the correct papers.

    b. The privateers attacked ships from countries not listed in their papers.

    c. The privateers were punished for attacking and plundering ships of enemy countries.

    d. The privateers did not have the necessary signatures on their papers.

MULTIPLE CHOICE COMPREHENSION

4

Points

(ACTIVITY G) Expository Writing—Summary

Writing Strategy—Summary

Step 1: LIST (List the details that are important enough to include in the summary.)
Step 2: CROSS OUT (Reread the details. Cross out any that you decide not to include.)
Step 3: CONNECT (Connect any details that could go into one sentence.)
Step 4: NUMBER (Number the details in a logical order.)
Step 5: WRITE (Write your summary.)
Step 6: EDIT (Revise and proofread your summary.)

Prompt: Write a summary of the most important information about pirates and piracy.

Planning Box
(topic)
(detail)
(detail)
(detail)
(detail)
(detail)
(detail)
(detail)
(detail)
(detail)
(detail)
(detail)

Directions: Write your summary on a separate piece of paper.

Rubric— Summary	Student or Partner Rating		Teacher Rating	
1. Did the author state the topic and the main idea in the first sentence?	Yes	Fix up	Yes	No
2. Did the author focus on important details?	Yes	Fix up	Yes	No
3. Did the author combine details in some of the sentences?	Yes	Fix up	Yes	No
4. Is the summary easy to understand?	Yes	Fix up	Yes	No
5. Did the author correctly spell words, particularly the words found in the article?	Yes	Fix up	Yes	No
6. Did the author use correct capitalization, capitalizing the first word in the sentence and proper names of people, places, and things?	Yes	Fix up	Yes	No
7. Did the author use correct punctuation, including a period at the end of each sentence?	Yes	Fix up	Yes	No

WRITING **7**

Points

(ACTIVITY A) *Vocabulary*

List 1: Tell

1. **Britain**   *n.* ▶ (an island nation in Europe; Great Britain, England)

2. **empire**   *n.* ▶ (a group of countries ruled by one country)

3. **mercantile**   *adj.* ▶ (relating to merchants)

4. **mercantilism**   *n.* ▶ (an economic system developed in France and Britain that stressed government control of the economy and trade)

List 2: Strategy Practice

1. **exploration**   *n.* ▶ (the act of traveling to an unknown place to learn about the place)

2. **acquisition**   *n.* ▶ (something you get that becomes your own)

3. **territory**   *n.* ▶ (any large area of land)

4. **possession**   *n.* ▶ (a territory that is under the rule of a foreign country)

5. **culminate**   *v.* ▶ (to reach the final point)

6. **independence**   *n.* ▶ (the state of not being ruled by another country)

7. **autonomy**   *n.* ▶ (independence or freedom)

8. **individual**   *adj.* ▶ (single and distinct)

9. **prevalent**   *adj.* ▶ (widespread)

10. **deposit**   *n.* ▶ (a natural layer of minerals in the earth)

TALLY ☐   VOCABULARY **5**
Points

List 3: Word Families

Family 1	value	n.	▶ (usefulness or importance)
	valuable	adj.	
	invaluable	adj.	

Family 2	inhabit	v.	▶ (to live in an area)
	inhabitant	n.	
	inhabitable	adj.	

Family 3	imperial	adj.	▶ (relating to an empire)
	imperialism	n.	
	imperialist	n.	

Family 4	expand	v.	▶ (to make larger)
	expansion	n.	
	expansive	adj.	

Family 5	colony	n.	▶ (a territory under the rule of another country)
	colonize	v.	
	colonization	n.	

(ACTIVITY B) *Spelling Dictation*

1.	4.
2.	5.
3.	6.

SPELLING 6 *Points*

ACTIVITY C *Background Knowledge*

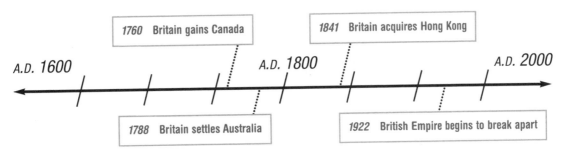

1760 Britain gains Canada

1841 Britain acquires Hong Kong

A.D. 1600   A.D. 1800   A.D. 2000

1788 Britain settles Australia

1922 British Empire begins to break apart

Like many European countries, Great Britain sought to expand its power and wealth by acquiring territories overseas. In this map, you can see the extent of Britain's territories (in black) as of 1914. Some of its largest possessions included Canada in North America, Australia, and India, on the continent of Asia. By examining the map, you will also notice some major possessions in Africa: Nigeria, Kenya, and South Africa. While these countries later became independent, they were all influenced by British culture.

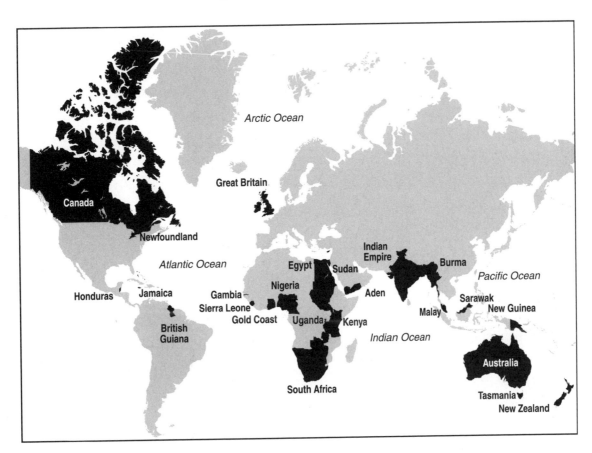

Map of the British Empire, Early 1900s

(ACTIVITY D) *Passage Reading and Comprehension*

The British Empire

	Britain, like many European nations, rushed to explore and expand during the
12	15th and 16th centuries. Explorers from England, France, Spain, and Portugal
23	sailed the seas, discovering new lands and people. Of all the countries that sought
37	new trade routes and new worlds, Britain alone turned its discoveries into a vast
51	empire that would continue well into the 1900s. The growth of the British
64	Empire had far-reaching effects on world politics and trade. (#1)
74	**A Mercantile Empire**
77	Initially, the expansion of the British Empire was based on *mercantilism*, or
89	trade. Britain realized that its own land had inadequate resources. It needed to
102	look to other lands for goods. The empire began with the exploration and
115	acquisition of the eastern coast of North America and with the West Indies, a
129	chain of islands stretching from the coast of Florida to South America. The
142	British traded goods for slaves in the West Indies and on the western coast of
157	Africa, where they also had settlements. These slaves were taken to southern
169	colonies, such as Virginia, Georgia, and South Carolina. The slaves supported
180	the growing of cotton and tobacco, goods that were then shipped back to
193	Britain, along with rum and sugar from the West Indies. (#2)
203	Meanwhile, the East India Company, a British company, had established a
214	stronghold in India. The company set up valuable trading posts for spices and
227	other goods. Eventually, the East India Company would come to rule India.
239	That rule would eventually be turned over to the British government. (#3)
250	**Expansion Continues**
252	The British Empire continued to expand for trade reasons. But there were
264	other reasons involved as well. Some of Britain's possessions in eastern Asia
276	were acquired as a result of several wars fought in that region in the 19th
291	century. Other countries were added for more unique reasons. Australia was
302	colonized as a penal colony (a place to send criminals for punishment). But 30
316	years after the first convicts came to Australia, Britain opened it to free citizens
330	and eventually stopped sending criminals there. South Africa, originally
339	colonized by the Dutch, was taken over by the British to try to keep the French
355	away. Once Britain had the land, they felt it was their duty to bring "civilized"
370	British culture to the land's inhabitants. British culture was prevalent throughout

| 381 | the world. By 1909, 20% of the land and 23% of the population of the world |
| 397 | belonged to the British Empire. (#4) |

Wealth Brings Power

402	
405	The British maintained and expanded their empire through trade and other
416	wealth-building. Many of their territories turned out to be rich in valuable
429	natural resources, adding to the wealth Britain would gain from colonies. West
441	Africa, for example, had rich deposits of gold and plenty of ivory. South Africa
455	had vast diamond mines, which are still the principal source of diamonds today.
468	The American colonies had furs, lumber, cotton, and tobacco. Britain was both
480	rich and powerful. (#5)

The Decline of the Empire

483	
488	This vast, wealthy empire covered much of the earth. People said that the
501	sun never set on the British Empire. Why then does it no longer exist? The
516	primary reason is that the individual territories got tired of being under British
529	rule. Many of them wanted self-government. In some cases—as in Canada and
543	Australia—the British government granted that autonomy. But in other cases,
554	the colonists fought for independence, as they did in America and India.
566	Gradually, Britain's possessions dwindled. This decline of a great empire
576	culminated with the return of Hong Kong to China in 1997. Today, Britain
589	retains only a few small territories, which are too tiny to govern themselves. (#6)
602	

ACTIVITY E *Fluency Building*

Cold Timing [ ] **Practice 1** [ ]

Practice 2 [ ] **Hot Timing** [ ]

ACTIVITY F *Comprehension Questions—*
Multiple Choice and Short Answer

Comprehension Strategy—Multiple Choice

Step 1: Read the item.

Step 2: Read all of the choices.

Step 3: Think about why each choice might be correct or incorrect. Check the article as needed.

Step 4: From the possible correct choices, select the best answer.

1. (Main Idea) **In the article, the statement "the sun never set on the British Empire" means that:**

   a. the British Empire never experienced the darkness of night.

   b. the glory of the British Empire was as bright as the sun.

   c. the British Empire was so wonderful that nothing could dim its greatness.

   d. the British Empire was large and worldwide.

2. (Cause and Effect) **What was the *major* reason Great Britain acquired territories overseas?**

   a. Great Britain wanted to obtain slaves who could work in the colonies.

   b. Great Britain wanted to bring its culture to other parts of the world.

   c. Great Britain wanted to expand its wealth and power.

   d. Great Britain wanted to trade in Asia.

3. (Main Idea) **If this article were given a new title, which would be best?**

   a. *British Rule in India, South Africa, and Australia*

   b. *The Rise and Fall of the British Empire*

   c. *Sunrise Over the British Empire*

   d. *The Growth of Trade*

4. (Cause and Effect) **Why did many of the territories of the British Empire want freedom from British rule?**

   a. They wanted to govern themselves.

   b. They wanted lower taxes.

   c. They wanted to select their own language and country name.

   d. They wanted to trade with countries other than Great Britain.

MULTIPLE CHOICE COMPREHENSION

4

Points

Comprehension Strategy—Short Answer

Step 1: Read the item.
Step 2: Turn the question into part of the answer and write it down.
Step 3: Think of the answer or locate the answer in the article.
Step 4: Complete your answer.

1. **Why was expansion of the British Empire initially based on trade?**
   The British Empire was initially based on trade because Britain wanted

   the power, wealth, and resources that could come from possessions

   overseas.

2. **What are some of the resources Britain found in its territories that helped to make it a wealthy country?**
   Some of the resources Britain found in its territories that helped to make

   it a wealthy country included gold, ivory, diamonds, furs, and lumber.

SHORT ANSWER COMPREHENSION **4** / 4

Points

(ACTIVITY G) *Expository Writing—Summary*

Writing Strategy—Summary

Step 1: LIST (List the details that are important enough to include in the summary.)
Step 2: CROSS OUT (Reread the details. Cross out any that you decide not to include.)
Step 3: CONNECT (Connect any details that could go into one sentence.)
Step 4: NUMBER (Number the details in a logical order.)
Step 5: WRITE (Write your summary.)
Step 6: EDIT (Revise and proofread your summary.)

Prompt: Write a summary of the information on the British Empire.

Planning Box
(topic)
(detail)
(detail)
(detail)
(detail)
(detail)
(detail)
(detail)
(detail)
(detail)
(detail)

Directions: Write your summary on a separate piece of paper.

Rubric— Summary	Student or Partner Rating		Teacher Rating	
1. Did the author state the topic and the main idea in the first sentence?	Yes	Fix up	Yes	No
2. Did the author focus on important details?	Yes	Fix up	Yes	No
3. Did the author combine details in some of the sentences?	Yes	Fix up	Yes	No
4. Is the summary easy to understand?	Yes	Fix up	Yes	No
5. Did the author correctly spell words, particularly the words found in the article?	Yes	Fix up	Yes	No
6. Did the author use correct capitalization, capitalizing the first word in the sentence and proper names of people, places, and things?	Yes	Fix up	Yes	No
7. Did the author use correct punctuation, including a period at the end of each sentence?	Yes	Fix up	Yes	No

WRITING

Points

(ACTIVITY A) *Vocabulary*

List 1: Tell

1.	**Mohandas Gandhi**	*n.*	▶ (a great human rights leader from India)
2.	**Mahatma**	*n.*	▶ (a title given to Gandhi that means "great-souled one")
3.	**campaign**	*n.*	▶ (a series of activities for some specific purpose)

List 2: Strategy Practice

1.	**compassion**	*n.*	▶ (sympathy for and a desire to help suffering people)
2.	**inferior**	*adj.*	▶ (lower in rank or importance)
3.	**compartment**	*n.*	▶ (an enclosed space, such as a room on a train)
4.	**passengers**	*n.*	▶ (people who travel in a vehicle)
5.	**incident**	*n.*	▶ (an event)
6.	**reputation**	*n.*	▶ (how people think of someone)
7.	**obligation**	*n.*	▶ (something a person must do)
8.	**comply**	*v.*	▶ (to act as requested)
9.	**relinquish**	*v.*	▶ (to give up)
10.	**associate**	*v.*	▶ (to connect in thought or memory)

TALLY [   ]   VOCABULARY

Points

List 3: Word Families

Family 1	justice	*n.*	▶ (fairness)
	injustice	*n.*	
	justification	*n.*	
Family 2	conduct	*v.*	▶ (to lead or guide)
	conductor	*n.*	
	conductible	*adj.*	
Family 3	prosecute	*v.*	▶ (to carry out a legal action against a person in a court of law)
	prosecution	*n.*	
	prosecutor	*n.*	
Family 4	equal	*adj.*	▶ (the same as)
	equality	*n.*	
	inequality	*n.*	
Family 5	dedicate	*v.*	▶ (to devote oneself to a purpose or person)
	dedication	*n.*	
	dedicator	*n.*	

(ACTIVITY B) *Spelling Dictation*

1.		**4.**	
2.		**5.**	
3.		**6.**	

SPELLING

6

Points

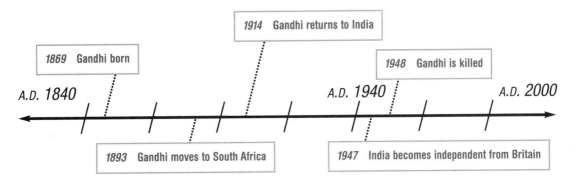

ACTIVITY C *Background Knowledge*

1914 Gandhi returns to India

1869 Gandhi born

A.D. *1840*

A.D. *1940*

A.D. *2000*

1948 Gandhi is killed

1893 Gandhi moves to South Africa

1947 India becomes independent from Britain

In the last article, we read about the expansion of the British Empire. Mahatma Gandhi was certainly a product of the British Empire. He was born in *India* in 1869, went to law school in *Great Britain,* lived in *South Africa* for more than 20 years, and returned to *India,* where he led a struggle for home rule and human rights until he was assassinated in 1948. Gandhi believed that nonviolent procedures should be used to gain human rights. These nonviolent procedures included non-cooperation by the people in forms of boycotting courts, resigning from government positions, and not attending school. These actions helped to propel India into independence from Great Britain.

However, Gandhi's career as a human rights leader did not start in India. Instead, it began during his years in South Africa. This is the period of his life discussed in this article.

Mohandas ("Mahatma") Gandhi

(ACTIVITY D) *Passage Reading and Comprehension*

Gandhi

	Mohandas Gandhi is known throughout the world for his compassion,
10	dedication to peace, and commitment to nonviolence. He enacted a great deal of
23	change in his lifetime and made life better for many people of India. His success
38	inspired other leaders, such as Martin Luther King Jr., to adopt nonviolent
50	resistance techniques in their own struggles against injustice. But Gandhi was not
62	born a leader. Specific events early in his life led him to that path. (#1)

	Becoming a Lawyer
76	
79	Gandhi attended University College in London, England, where he studied
89	successfully to become a lawyer. This training in law would provide an important
102	base of knowledge for Gandhi throughout his lifetime. When he completed
113	school, he returned to India and attempted to start a law practice in Bombay.
127	He was not very successful. Few clients approached him; he was not making
140	enough money to live. So when an offer came to work as a legal advisor in South
157	Africa, he gladly accepted it. (#2)

	South Africa
162	
164	Like India, South Africa was still under British rule when Gandhi moved
176	there in 1893. In South Africa, Gandhi realized that the large numbers of
189	Indians (people from India) who were settled there were looked down upon as
202	racial outcasts. South African whites considered the Indians inferior just because
213	they were Indian. One day, Gandhi boarded a train with a first-class ticket in his
229	hand. But when he sat down in the compartment, a white passenger complained
242	about the presence of a dark-skinned man in first class. The conductor ordered
256	him to move back to third class. When Gandhi refused, because he had
269	purchased a first-class ticket, the conductor threw him and his luggage off the
283	train. He sat through a cold winter night in a waiting room, trying to decide
298	whether he should stay and fulfill his obligations to his law client or return to
313	India. He decided to stay. (#3)

	Passive Resistance
318	
320	Later, on the same journey, Gandhi had to travel by stagecoach. The
332	conductor made Gandhi sit outside of the stagecoach box while he sat inside with
346	the white passengers. Afraid of being thrown off and getting stranded, Gandhi

358	complied. But when the same conductor ordered Gandhi to move out of his seat
372	and sit on the dirty footboard, Gandhi refused. The conductor was very angry
385	and hit Gandhi repeatedly, trying to force him off the stagecoach. Gandhi was not
399	willing to fight back, and he was not willing to concede. Finally, some of the
414	other passengers made the conductor stop. Gandhi remained in his seat. (#4)

Becoming a Leader

425	
428	These incidents awoke Gandhi's awareness to the terrible racial injustices
438	being done in South Africa. He began to try to organize his fellow Indians and
453	others who disagreed with the government's actions. He made speeches and
464	wrote petitions and pamphlets. People in Britain and India began to become
476	aware of what was happening in South Africa. (#5)

Nonviolent Resistance

484	
486	As Gandhi's campaign wore on, people who did not approve of the changes
499	he was trying to enact often confronted him. On one occasion, he was attacked
513	by an angry mob of people and nearly killed. But he refused to prosecute his
528	attackers, saying that they would find their own way to the truth. He began to be
544	known as much for his love and compassion for his enemies as for his political
559	successes. (#6)

The Mahatma

560	
562	As his reputation for compassion grew, Gandhi became known as the
573	*Mahatma,* or "great-souled one." He relinquished the lifestyle of a lawyer and
586	began to live the simple, sparse life that we associate with Gandhi today. Out of
601	these experiences in South Africa, he developed his practice of *satyagraha,* or
613	nonviolent resistance to injustice. His experiences with hatred, injustice, and
623	prejudice led him to become a great leader for peace and equality in India, his
638	homeland, and around the world. (#7)
643	

(ACTIVITY E) *Fluency Building*

Cold Timing		**Practice 1**	
Practice 2		**Hot Timing**	

(ACTIVITY F) *Comprehension Questions— Multiple Choice and Short Answer*

Comprehension Strategy—Multiple Choice

Step 1: Read the item.
Step 2: Read all of the choices.
Step 3: Think about why each choice might be correct or incorrect. Check the article as needed.
Step 4: From the possible correct choices, select the best answer.

1. (Vocabulary) **What did the author mean with this statement: "Mahatma Gandhi was certainly a *product* of the British Empire."**
    a. Gandhi's ideas were the same as the leaders of countries in the British Empire.
    b. The British Empire made Gandhi a political leader because he earned a law degree in Great Britain.
    c. Gandhi learned from his experiences in three countries of the British Empire: India, Great Britain, and South Africa.
    d. Gandhi's goals were the same as those who wrote the laws of the British Empire.

2. (Cause and Effect) **Why did the conductor try to force Gandhi off the stagecoach?**
    a. There was great prejudice against people of color in South Africa.
    b. Gandhi had failed to pay the same fare as the other passengers.
    c. The conductor did not realize that Gandhi was a lawyer and deserved respect.
    d. Gandhi was not a British citizen.

3. (Vocabulary) **What do you think the heading *Passive Resistance* means?**
    a. Resistance that is "in passing" (only temporary).
    b. Resistance that does not involve passing over other people.
    c. Resistance that does not involve action, such as fighting.
    d. Resistance that involves getting other people to protect you.

4. (Main Idea) **If Gandhi were given an award, which of these titles would be best?**
    a. *Nonviolent Peace Seeker*
    b. *Leader of the British Empire*
    c. *Beloved Leader of Bombay*
    d. *Recognized Lawyer*

MULTIPLE CHOICE COMPREHENSION **4**

Points

Comprehension Strategy—Short Answer

Step 1: Read the item.
Step 2: Turn the question into part of the answer and write it down.
Step 3: Think of the answer or locate the answer in the article.
Step 4: Complete your answer.

1. Why was life difficult for the Indians who lived in South Africa?

_____

_____

_____

_____

2. What kinds of nonviolent actions did Gandhi support?

_____

_____

_____

_____

SHORT ANSWER COMPREHENSION **4**

Points

(ACTIVITY G) *Expository Writing—Extended Response*

Writing Strategy—Extended Response

Step 1: LIST (List the reasons for your position. For each reason, explain with details.)
Step 2: CROSS OUT (Reread your reasons and details. Cross out any that you decide not to include.)
Step 3: CONNECT (Connect any details that could go into one sentence.)
Step 4: NUMBER (Number the reasons in a logical order.)
Step 5: WRITE (Write your response.)
Step 6: EDIT (Revise and proofread your response.)

Prompt: Describe some of the parts of Gandhi's life that led him to be a great leader for peace.

Example Extended Response Plan

Planning Box
(position) *Many factors in Gandhi's life led him to be a great leader for peace.*
(reason) *– lived throughout the British Empire*
(explain) *– born in India*
– also lived in South Africa and Great Britain
(reason) *– knew what it was like to be a racial outcast*
(explain) *– conductor told him to sit with other dark-skinned people in third-class section on the train*
– thrown off the train when he refused
(reason) *– responded to violence with nonviolence*
(explain) *– hit repeatedly on the stagecoach*
– refused to fight back
(reason) *– organized people who disagreed with the government*
(explain) *– wrote pamphlets and petitions*
– made speeches
– people became more aware of what was happening

Directions: Write your extended response on a separate piece of paper.

Example Extended Response

Many factors in Gandhi's life led him to become a great leader for peace. First, he knew what it was like to be a racial outcast. On one trip, he was told to sit with other dark-skinned people in third class, even though he had a first-class ticket. When he refused, he was thrown off the train. Another factor is that he responded to violence with nonviolence. He was once hit repeatedly for refusing to move onto the footboard of a stagecoach, but he would not fight back. Finally, Gandhi organized people who disagreed with the government. He wrote pamphlets and petitions, and he made speeches. He made people more aware of what was happening in regard to the government and civil rights.

Rubric— Extended Response	Student or Partner Rating		Teacher Rating	
1. Did the author tell his/her position in the first sentence?	Yes	Fix up	Yes	No
2. Did the author include at least three **strong, logical** reasons for his/her position?	Yes	Fix up	Yes	No
3. Did the author provide a **strong, logical** explanation for each of his/her reasons?	Yes	Fix up	Yes	No
4. Is the response easy to understand?	Yes	Fix up	Yes	No
5. Did the author correctly spell words, particularly the words found in the article?	Yes	Fix up	Yes	No
6. Did the author use correct capitalization, capitalizing the first word in the sentence and proper names of people, places, and things?	Yes	Fix up	Yes	No
7. Did the author use correct punctuation, including a period at the end of each sentence?	Yes	Fix up	Yes	No

WRITING 7 *Points*

ACTIVITY A *Vocabulary*

List 1: Tell

1.	**Sybil Ludington**	*n.* ▶	(a 16-year-old who warned neighbors)
2.	**Susanna Boiling**	*n.* ▶	(a teenager who crossed a river alone)
3.	**Lydia Barrington Darragh**	*n.* ▶	(a woman who warned George Washington)
4.	**Anne Kennedy**	*n.* ▶	(a woman who organized an attack)
5.	**Margaret Warne**	*n.* ▶	(a woman doctor who didn't charge a fee to patients)
6.	**Prudence Wright**	*n.* ▶	(a woman who commanded a regiment)
7.	**Paul Revere**	*n.* ▶	(a man who warned of British attack)
8.	**General Lafayette**	*n.* ▶	(an army general)

List 2: Strategy Practice

1.	**invasion**	*n.* ▶	(the entrance of an army into a country)
2.	**regiment**	*n.* ▶	(a military unit of an army)
3.	**occupation**	*n.* ▶	(a job; a profession)
4.	**declaration**	*n.* ▶	(a formal statement; an announcement)
5.	**representation**	*n.* ▶	(the function of speaking for a group of people)
6.	**disobedience**	*n.* ▶	(failure to follow an order)
7.	**commandeer**	*v.* ▶	(to take; to seize)
8.	**capture**	*v.* ▶	(to take by force)
9.	**official**	*adj.* ▶	(relating to an office or position of duty)
10.	**capacity**	*n.* ▶	(a position; a function; a role)

TALLY ☐   VOCABULARY 5

Points

List 3: Word Families

Family 1	**independent**	*adj.* ▶ (not controlled by others)
	independently	*adv.*
	independence	*n.*

Family 2	**colony**	*n.* ▶ (territory under the control of another country)
	colonial	*adj.*
	colonist	*n.*

Family 3	**produce**	*v.* ▶ (to make)
	product	*n.*
	production	*n.*

Family 4	**participate**	*v.* ▶ (to take part in an activity)
	participated	*v.*
	participation	*n.*

Family 5	**revolt**	*v.* ▶ (to break away from or rise up against an authority)
	revolution	*n.*
	revolutionary	*adj.*

(ACTIVITY B) *Spelling Dictation*

1.	4.
2.	5.
3.	6.

SPELLING 6 *Points*

ACTIVITY C *Background Knowledge*

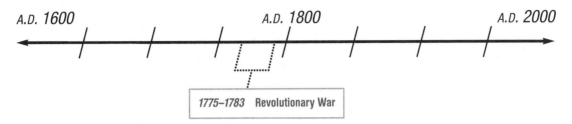

A.D. *1600*   A.D. *1800*   A.D. *2000*

1775–1783   Revolutionary War

In this article, you will read about the role of women in the Revolutionary War, which was fought from 1775 to 1783. You probably wonder why Americans decided to fight this war. In the years leading up to the war, the British ruled the people in the American colonies without representation. The British expected the colonists to pay a lot of taxes and to follow laws they didn't believe in. The colonists made a declaration of independence and fought the British to become independent. Many American women helped defeat the British.

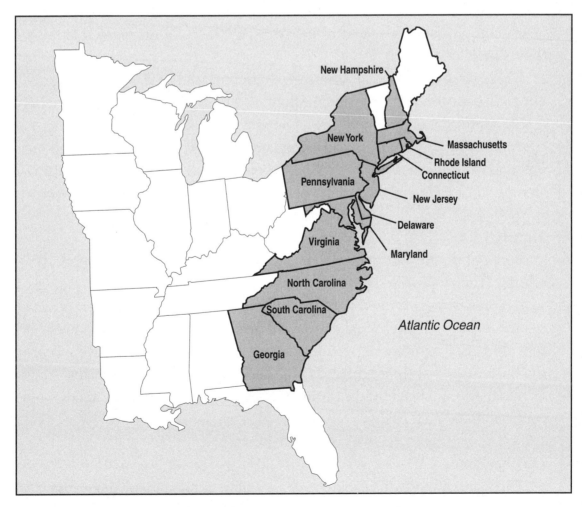

The Original 13 American Colonies, 1775

(**ACTIVITY D**) *Passage Reading and Comprehension*

Women in the American Revolution

	The Revolutionary War brings many images to mind. You might think of
12	colonial men fighting against the British men in their red coats. Or, you might
26	think of George Washington and other founding fathers. But did you know that
39	there were many women who played a role in the American Revolution as well?
53	They were soldiers, spies, and nurses, and they worked hard to fight for
66	independence from the British. (#1)
70	**Warnings**
71	Most Americans know the story of Paul Revere's ride through the town,
83	warning of British invasion. But few people have heard of 16-year-old Sybil
97	Ludington. On a dark night in 1777, she rode through her Connecticut town to
111	rouse, or awaken, her neighbors. She had witnessed the British attack of a
124	nearby supply house. Because of her warning, the colonists were able to save
137	their supply depot. (#2)
140	There were other young American women who braved danger to warn of
152	impending British attacks. Susanna Boiling, a teenager, crossed a river alone one
164	night to inform General Lafayette of an attack the British were planning. Lydia
177	Barrington Darragh, a 48-year-old woman who had nine children, spied on a
191	meeting of British commanders. She traveled across enemy lines to notify
202	George Washington of the British plan to attack his soldiers. (#3)
212	**Supply Lines**
214	Some of the Revolutionary women focused their attention on supporting war
225	efforts. Women provided passing colonial troops with food, shelter, candles, and
236	soap. Some women formed patriotic societies. Some of these societies raised
247	money to purchase boots and gunpowder for their soldiers. Some sewed and
259	sent shirts, socks, quilts, and bandages for troops. Some women even took over
272	the businesses that their husbands ran. They became butchers, bakers, millers,
283	fishmongers, and blacksmiths during the war so that production needs would
294	continue to be met. (#4)
298	**Disobedience**
299	During the war, British soldiers would often commandeer (take) farms, crop
310	supplies, or homes in order to supply their armies. A number of women refused

324	to cooperate with the British. Some women burned their crops, preventing the
336	British from taking them. Others defended their own homes against British
347	occupation. Anne Kennedy, a woman from South Carolina, organized an attack
358	against British forces that were attempting to take her home and her crops. She
372	was wounded in the battle, but the British fled. (#5)

381	**Nurses and Soldiers**
384	The colonial armies required nurses to help tend the sick and the wounded.
397	Congress granted them one nurse for every ten patients. The nurses were paid
410	monthly and given one food ration per day. Other women participated in a less
424	official capacity. Margaret Warne was a physician from New Jersey. During the war,
437	she would ride through the country and aid soldiers and their families at no charge.
452	Some women fought on the battlefields. They fought alongside their
462	husbands, helping them to clean and load cannons or carry water. Many women
475	who fought as soldiers disguised themselves as men in order to enlist in the
489	army. Prudence Wright, from Massachusetts, actually commanded a regiment
498	entirely made up of women dressed as men. They defended their town and
511	captured a British messenger and his plans. (#6)

518	**Founding Fathers . . . and Women, Too**
523	Women provided a great deal of support during the Revolutionary War, both
535	on the battlefield and back at home. Although their stories are not as well
549	known as their male counterparts' stories, women played important roles in the
561	war effort. Together, colonial men and women defeated the British and helped
573	to shape America. (#7)
576	

(ACTIVITY E) *Fluency Building*

| Cold Timing | | Practice 1 | |
| Practice 2 | | Hot Timing | |

(ACTIVITY F) *Comprehension Questions— Multiple Choice and Short Answer*

Comprehension Strategy—Multiple Choice

Step 1: Read the item.

Step 2: Read all of the choices.

Step 3: Think about why each choice might be correct or incorrect. Check the article as needed.

Step 4: From the possible correct choices, select the best answer.

1. (Vocabulary) **What two words from the article are synonyms?**

    a. arouse and **awaken**

    b. warning and **attack**

    c. ration and **capacity**

    d. witness and **notify**

2. (Main Idea) **What is the main idea of this article?**

    a. During the Revolutionary War, women served as nurses and soldiers.

    b. Women, as well as men, played important roles in the Revolutionary War.

    c. The colonists defeated the British in the Revolutionary War.

    d. Some women, disguised as men, actually fought as soldiers in the Revolutionary War.

3. (Vocabulary) **Read this sentence from the passage: "There were other young American women who braved danger to warn of *impending* British attacks." What does the word *impending* mean?**

    a. dangerous

    b. about to end

    c. about to happen

    d. deadly

4. (Cause and Effect) **Why did the women who fought as soldiers disguise themselves?**

    a. They wanted to go behind the British lines.

    b. Male soldiers were less likely to be killed in battle.

    c. Only men were allowed to enlist in the army.

    d. The soldiers' uniforms were more comfortable than the nurses' clothing.

MULTIPLE CHOICE COMPREHENSION ◢ **4**

Points

Comprehension Strategy—Short Answer

Step 1: Read the item.
Step 2: Turn the question into part of the answer and write it down.
Step 3: Think of the answer or locate the answer in the article.
Step 4: Complete your answer.

1. **What conclusions about the Revolutionary War does the author of this article want you to reach?**

   _____

   _____

   _____

   _____

2. **What were three of the most dangerous things women did during the Revolutionary War?**

   _____

   _____

   _____

   _____

SHORT ANSWER COMPREHENSION 4

Points

ACTIVITY G *Expository Writing—Extended Response*

Writing Strategy—Extended Response

Step 1: LIST (List the reasons for your position. For each reason, explain with details.)
Step 2: CROSS OUT (Reread your reasons and details. Cross out any that you decide not to include.)
Step 3: CONNECT (Connect any details that could go into one sentence.)
Step 4: NUMBER (Number the reasons in a logical order.)
Step 5: WRITE (Write your response.)
Step 6: EDIT (Revise and proofread your response.)

Prompt: Explain why women's roles were as important as men's roles in defeating the British during the Revolutionary War.

Planning Box
(position)
(reason)
(explain)
(reason)
(explain)
(reason)
(explain)
(reason)
(explain)

Directions: Write your extended response on a separate piece of paper.

Rubric— Extended Response	Student or Partner Rating		Teacher Rating	
1. Did the author tell his/her position in the first sentence?	Yes	Fix up	Yes	No
2. Did the author include at least three **strong, logical** reasons for his/her position?	Yes	Fix up	Yes	No
3. Did the author provide a **strong, logical** explanation for each of his/her reasons?	Yes	Fix up	Yes	No
4. Is the response easy to understand?	Yes	Fix up	Yes	No
5. Did the author correctly spell words, particularly the words found in the article?	Yes	Fix up	Yes	No
6. Did the author use correct capitalization, capitalizing the first word in the sentence and proper names of people, places, and things?	Yes	Fix up	Yes	No
7. Did the author use correct punctuation, including a period at the end of each sentence?	Yes	Fix up	Yes	No

WRITING   **7**

Points

(ACTIVITY A) *Vocabulary*

List 1: Tell

1. **the Senate**   *n.* ▶ (the upper house of the U.S. Congress that has two people from each state)

2. **senators**   *n.* ▶ (members of the U.S. Senate)

3. **Supreme Court**   *n.* ▶ (the highest court in the U.S.)

4. **justices**   *n.* ▶ (the Supreme Court judges)

5. **agencies**   *n.* ▶ (governmental offices that help run things)

6. **system**   *n.* ▶ (a set of beliefs, facts, rules, and laws)

7. **notifying**   *v.* ▶ (letting someone know about something)

8. **democracy**   *n.* ▶ (a government ruled by the people, even if through representation)

List 2: Strategy Practice

1. **comprise**   *v.* ▶ (to include or consist of)

2. **population**   *n.* ▶ (the number of people living in an area)

3. **Constitution**   *n.* ▶ (the document outlining the plan for the U.S. government)

4. **unconstitutional**   *adj.* ▶ (not in keeping with the U.S. Constitution)

5. **nominate**   *v.* ▶ (to appoint to a job or office)

6. **limitation**   *n.* ▶ (something that keeps something else from happening)

7. **responsibility**   *n.* ▶ (a job or duty)

8. **impeachment**   *n.* ▶ (the act of bringing a formal charge against someone to remove that person from office)

9. **similarly**   *adv.* ▶ (like something else)

10. **presidential**   *adj.* ▶ (having to do with the president of a country or organization)

TALLY ☐   VOCABULARY 5 *Points*

List 3: Word Families

Family 1	**legislate**	v.	▶ (to make a law)
	legislative	adj.	
	legislation	n.	

Family 2	**execute**	v.	▶ (to carry out; to accomplish)
	executive	n.	
	execution	n.	

Family 3	**judge**	n.	▶ (someone who hears and decides cases in a court of law)
	judicial	adj.	
	judiciary	n.	

Family 4	**govern**	v.	▶ (to rule by right of authority)
	governor	n.	
	government	n.	

Family 5	**represent**	v.	▶ (to serve as the speaker for others)
	representative	n.	
	representation	n.	

(ACTIVITY B) *Spelling Dictation*

1.	4.
2.	5.
3.	6.

SPELLING 6 *Points*

(ACTIVITY C) *Background Knowledge*

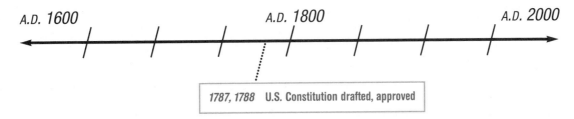

A.D. *1600*   A.D. *1800*   A.D. *2000*

1787, 1788   U.S. Constitution drafted, approved

This article tells about the three branches of government described in the U.S. Constitution, which was drafted in 1787 and approved by the original 13 states in 1788. After the colonists defeated the British, they needed a way to rule themselves, so they created a document and called it the Constitution. The colonists wanted to create a government that was different from what they experienced under British rule. For example, they wanted to make sure that power belonged to the people. So, they wrote a Bill of Rights, which listed the rights of individuals that cannot be taken away by the government, and they created a system of representation. The colonists also made sure that the powers granted to any of the three branches of government were balanced against each other.

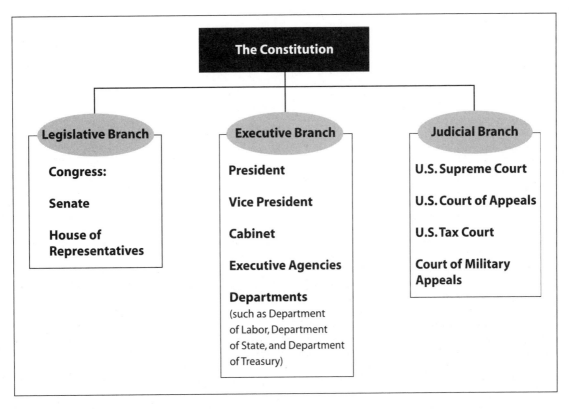

Diagram of U.S. Government Branches

ACTIVITY D *Passage Reading and Comprehension*

Branches of the United States Government

	When the colonists drew up the Constitution, in which they constructed a
12	system of government, they wanted to be sure that the government was strong.
25	But, they also wanted to make sure that the power remained balanced. They
38	finally decided that they would create a government that has three branches:
50	legislative, executive, and judicial. (#1)
54	**Legislative Branch**
56	Article 1 of the Constitution is concerned with the legislative branch of the
69	government, which is the system of representation the colonists created. The
80	primary function of the legislative branch, or Congress, is to enact legislation, or
93	make laws, for the country. Congress is comprised of two groups: the Senate and
107	the House of Representatives. Each state has two senators who are elected by
120	the people. One-third of the Senate seats come up for election every two years.
135	This way, the Senate is never totally new. The House of Representatives is much
149	larger, because each state elects a certain number of representatives based on its
162	population. The greater the number of people living in a state, the higher the
176	number of representatives. Elections for representatives are held every two
186	years. (#2)
187	**Executive Branch**
189	The president, vice president, Cabinet members, and executive agencies are
199	all part of the executive branch of government. The executive branch was
211	established in Article 2 of the Constitution. It is the duty of the executive branch
226	of government to make sure that the nation follows its laws. The president acts
240	as the commander-in-chief of the armed forces. The president is also
253	responsible for notifying Congress about the well-being of the country and can
266	request a special session of Congress, if necessary. In addition, the president has
279	the power to pardon federal criminals. The president is limited to two four-year
293	terms in office. (#3)
296	**Judicial Branch**
298	Established by Article 3 of the Constitution, the judicial branch is
309	responsible for deciding if the laws enacted by Congress and by the states are
323	constitutional, or in line with the Constitution. The primary arm of the judicial

336	branch of government is the Supreme Court. The Supreme Court was created
348	according to the Constitution. Later, Congress also created several lower federal
359	courts. The Supreme Court has nine members, called *justices.* These justices are
371	nominated by the president, but must be approved by Congress. Justices do not
384	have any term limitations; once they are appointed, they hold office for life or
398	until they retire. (#4)

401	**Checks and Balances**
404	The government's responsibilities and powers were spread over three
413	different branches to ensure that no one person or agency gains too much
426	power. Therefore, within the system the United States currently has, a number
438	of checks and balances are built in. *Veto power* is one example. This means that
453	if Congress votes to pass a law, the president has the power to keep the law from
470	happening by vetoing that law. Then, if Congress can muster a two-thirds vote in
485	favor of the law, it can override the president's veto. (#5)
495	Another example of checks and balances is *impeachment.* If the president
506	abuses official power or breaks the law in some way, Congress and the Supreme
520	Court have the power to remove the president from office. Both groups in
533	Congress must vote in agreement for presidential impeachment to take place.
544	Similarly, Supreme Court justices can be impeached if they abuse their position.
556	The Supreme Court can also declare laws or presidential actions
566	unconstitutional. (#6)
567	The founding fathers remembered what they didn't like about being under
578	British rule. By splitting the power of the United States government, they
590	helped to ensure that the leadership of the country would be balanced. They
603	created a system of checks and balances to make sure that no one part of the
619	government could become too powerful. The founding fathers established rule
629	by representation and listed individuals' rights on paper, thus forming the
640	foundation of a democracy that has been operating for more than 200 years. (#7)
653	

(ACTIVITY E) *Fluency Building*

Cold Timing [   ]   **Practice 1** [   ]

Practice 2 [   ]   **Hot Timing** [   ]

(ACTIVITY F) *Comprehension Questions—*
Multiple Choice and Short Answer

Comprehension Strategy—Multiple Choice

Step 1: Read the item.
Step 2: Read all of the choices.
Step 3: Think about why each choice might be correct or incorrect. Check the article as needed.
Step 4: From the possible correct choices, select the best answer.

1. (Vocabulary) **What does the term "checks and balances" mean when referring to the U.S. government?**
   a. An accounting system in which each checkbook is balanced.
   b. A system in which the voters can check the actions of politicians.
   c. A system of government in which the president can override legislative actions.
   d. A system in which power is divided among three branches of government, and safeguards are built in to ensure that no branch has too much power.

2. (Cause and Effect) **Why did the Constitution form three branches of government rather than just one?**
   a. So that more people would have government jobs.
   b. So that the president could keep a law from happening by vetoing the law.
   c. So that no one person or branch would have too much power.
   d. So that the president could be impeached, if necessary.

3. (Compare and Contrast) **How are the Senate and the House of Representatives the same?**
   a. The length of time representatives and senators serve.
   b. The number of people in each group.
   c. The law-making function.
   d. How often seats come up for election.

4. (Main Idea) **Which of these similes best describes the government established by the U.S. Constitution?**
   a. The American government is like a tree with strong branches and a strong root system.
   b. The American government is like an umbrella that opens to protect its citizens.
   c. The American government is like a mansion with hidden rooms.
   d. The American government is like apple pie à la mode (with ice cream).

MULTIPLE CHOICE COMPREHENSION

4

Points

Comprehension Strategy—Short Answer

Step 1: Read the item.
Step 2: Turn the question into part of the answer and write it down.
Step 3: Think of the answer or locate the answer in the article.
Step 4: Complete your answer.

1. How is the Senate different from the House of Representatives?

_____

_____

_____

_____

2. How do Supreme Court justices get their jobs?

_____

_____

_____

_____

SHORT ANSWER COMPREHENSION
Points

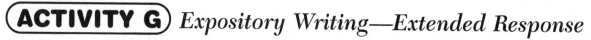

(ACTIVITY G) *Expository Writing—Extended Response*

Writing Strategy—Extended Response

Step 1: LIST (List the reasons for your position. For each reason, explain with details.)

Step 2: CROSS OUT (Reread your reasons and details. Cross out any that you decide not to include.)

Step 3: CONNECT (Connect any details that could go into one sentence.)

Step 4: NUMBER (Number the reasons in a logical order.)

Step 5: WRITE (Write your response.)

Step 6: EDIT (Revise and proofread your response.)

Prompt: If you could choose a job in one branch of the U.S. government, tell which branch and why.

Planning Box
(position)
(reason)
(explain)
(reason)
(explain)
(reason)
(explain)
(reason)
(explain)

Directions: Write your extended response on a separate piece of paper.

Rubric— Extended Response	Student or Partner Rating		Teacher Rating	
1. Did the author tell his/her position in the first sentence?	Yes	Fix up	Yes	No
2. Did the author include at least three **strong, logical** reasons for his/her position?	Yes	Fix up	Yes	No
3. Did the author provide a **strong, logical** explanation for each of his/her reasons?	Yes	Fix up	Yes	No
4. Is the response easy to understand?	Yes	Fix up	Yes	No
5. Did the author correctly spell words, particularly the words found in the article?	Yes	Fix up	Yes	No
6. Did the author use correct capitalization, capitalizing the first word in the sentence and proper names of people, places, and things?	Yes	Fix up	Yes	No
7. Did the author use correct punctuation, including a period at the end of each sentence?	Yes	Fix up	Yes	No

WRITING 7

Points

(ACTIVITY A) *Vocabulary*

List 1: Tell

1. **guarantee**   *v.* ▶ (to promise that something will happen)
2. **aliens**   *n.* ▶ (people who are not citizens of the country in which they are living)
3. **privileges**   *n.* ▶ (special rights)
4. **society**   *n.* ▶ (a group of people)
5. **allegiance**   *n.* ▶ (loyalty to a government)

List 2: Strategy Practice

1. **automatically**   *adv.* ▶ (done without a person's control)
2. **citizen**   *n.* ▶ (a person born in a country or one who chooses to become a member of a country by law)
3. **citizenship**   *n.* ▶ (the state of having the rights and duties of a citizen)
4. **opportunity**   *n.* ▶ (a good chance to advance oneself)
5. **territory**   *n.* ▶ (a part of the United States that does not have the status of a state)
6. **nationals**   *n.* ▶ (people who are members of a nation)
7. **democratic**   *adj.* ▶ (believing all people are politically equal)
8. **generally**   *adv.* ▶ (in most cases; usually)
9. **circumstances**   *n.* ▶ (events that affect other events)
10. **particular**   *adj.* ▶ (specific)

TALLY   VOCABULARY 5

Points

List 3: Word Families

Family 1	natural	*adj.* ▶ (belonging to from birth)
	naturalized	*adj.*
	naturalization	*n.*

Family 2	immigrate	*v.* ▶ (to enter a country in which one was not born in order to make a home)
	immigrants	*n.*
	immigration	*n.*

Family 3	responsible	*adj.* ▶ (having a job or duty)
	responsibility	*n.*
	responsibilities	*n.*

Family 4	apply	*v.* ▶ (to make an application or request for a position or job)
	applicant	*n.*
	application	*n.*

Family 5	volunteer	*v.* ▶ (to do something of one's own free will)
	voluntary	*adj.*
	voluntarily	*adv.*

ACTIVITY B *Spelling Dictation*

1.	4.
2.	5.
3.	6.

SPELLING 6

Points

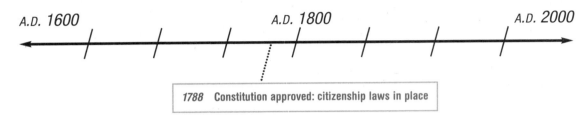

ACTIVITY C *Background Knowledge*

A.D. *1600*   A.D. *1800*   A.D. *2000*

1788 Constitution approved: citizenship laws in place

When a person is born in a particular country, the person is considered a citizen of that country. However, some people choose to move to another country to join family members or to obtain work. When people go to a new country, they may wish to become citizens of that new country. This may be an easy or difficult process, depending on the country and the person's circumstances. In this article, you will learn about the citizenship process that has been used in the United States since 1788. In the United States, citizens have full legal and political rights. Full citizenship brings with it all of the protections and privileges guaranteed by the Constitution.

© 2003 www.clipart.com

Immigrants in New York, Late 1800s

(ACTIVITY D) *Passage Reading and Comprehension*

United States Citizenship

	People from all over the world come to the United States of America to live.
15	They come to find opportunity, to seek freedom, or to be with family. People
29	come to the United States because they know that U.S. citizens are guaranteed
42	certain rights, such as the right to believe and practice any religion they want or
57	the right to freedom of speech. But just because someone moves here from
70	another country doesn't mean he or she is automatically a citizen. If a person
84	was not born in the United States, or if you were born to a United States citizen
101	living in a foreign country, it is necessary to apply for citizenship. (#1)

113	**Naturalization**
114	When people from a foreign country want to become citizens of the United
127	States, they must go through a process called *naturalization*. There are three
139	steps to this process. First, they must file an application with the government.
152	This application asks them for information about their background. They must
163	also provide photographs and legal documents. The government takes the
173	applicant's fingerprints. (#2)
175	Second, the applicants must take a test. This test asks questions about United
188	States history and government. Applicants can take classes to help them study
200	for the test. They also have to take an English test to make sure they know the
217	language well. (#3)
219	Lastly, the applicants must appear before a judge. The judge asks each of
232	them why they want to be a citizen and if they are willing to take an oath of
250	allegiance, or loyalty, to the United States. After the applicant answers, the
262	judge decides whether or not he or she may become a citizen. (#4)

274	**Aliens' and Nationals' Rights**
278	People who have just moved to the United States from a foreign country are
292	known as *aliens*. This means they live here, but they are not full citizens of the
308	country. They have some of the rights of a citizen, but there are some rights—
323	such as voting and federal work—that they cannot have. However, once they go
337	through naturalization, naturalized citizens can have jobs with the government,
347	obtain a passport from the United States, and request that family members be
360	allowed to immigrate to the United States. (#5)

367	People who live in American territories (such as Puerto Rico, Guam, or the
380	Virgin Islands) are known as *nationals*. They share all of the legal rights of U.S.
395	citizens but have different political rights. For example, they are not represented
407	in Congress, and they cannot run for president. (#6)
415	**Citizens' Responsibilities**
417	Citizens have many rights, but they also have responsibilities. In the United
429	States, a citizen may be called to be on a jury. A jury helps decide the outcome
446	of a court case. If citizens are requested for jury duty, they have to be on the
463	jury for as long as the court case continues. (#7)
472	American citizens also have a responsibility to exercise their right to vote.
484	The democratic process by which this country is governed depends on
495	individual involvement. By voting, Americans can support or disagree with
505	policies or leaders. Participation in local government is also a good way to show
519	responsibility as a citizen. (#8)
523	Male citizens may be drafted into the military during times of war. If the
537	government deems it necessary, then citizens must help defend the country.
548	During peacetime, all citizens, male or female, may enlist voluntarily in the
560	military. (#9)
561	Finally, all citizens are responsible for upholding the laws of their
572	communities, states, and nation. This includes paying income tax and other taxes
584	to state and federal agencies and respecting the rights of other citizens. Each
597	citizen must do his or her part to help the society to continue to run smoothly.
613	Becoming a citizen of the United States is a great privilege, but it is also a great
630	responsibility. (#10)
631	

(ACTIVITY E) *Fluency Building*

Cold Timing [ ]　　　　**Practice 1** [ ]

Practice 2 [ ]　　　　**Hot Timing** [ ]

(ACTIVITY F) *Comprehension Questions—*
Multiple Choice and Short Answer

Comprehension Strategy—Multiple Choice

Step 1: Read the item.

Step 2: Read all of the choices.

Step 3: Think about why each choice might be correct or incorrect. Check the article as needed.

Step 4: From the possible correct choices, select the best answer.

1. (Vocabulary) **What two words from the article are synonyms?**

  a. application and **document**

  b. guarantee and **automatic**

  c. privileges and **rights**

  d. rights and **responsibilities**

2. (Compare and Contrast) **What right does a U.S. citizen have that an alien does *not* have?**

  a. The right to practice their religion.

  b. The right to vote.

  c. The right to speak freely about political issues.

  d. The right to purchase things they need.

3. (Main Idea) **Which statement gives the best summary of this article?**

  a. Aliens do not have the same rights as citizens. They cannot vote, run for office, or hold a U.S. passport.

  b. People may immigrate to the U.S. to be with their family, to seek freedom, or to search for economic opportunities.

  c. To become a naturalized citizen, you must apply, take a test, and appear in front of a judge.

  d. When you become an American citizen, you gain certain rights (such as the right to vote and have a U.S. passport), but you also gain responsibilities (such as serving on a jury).

4. (Vocabulary) **Which sentence *best* expresses the relationship between the words *application* and *applicant*?**

  a. An applicant fills out an application.

  b. An applicant receives people's applications.

  c. An application informs an applicant.

  d. An application lists an applicant.

MULTIPLE CHOICE COMPREHENSION

Points

Comprehension Strategy—Short Answer

Step 1: Read the item.
Step 2: Turn the question into part of the answer and write it down.
Step 3: Think of the answer or locate the answer in the article.
Step 4: Complete your answer.

1. **What three steps are necessary to become a naturalized citizen of the United States?**

_____

_____

_____

_____

2. **How do the rights of aliens differ from the rights of U.S. citizens?**

_____

_____

_____

_____

SHORT ANSWER COMPREHENSION
Points

ACTIVITY G *Expository Writing—Extended Response*

Writing Strategy—Extended Response

Step 1: LIST (List the reasons for your position. For each reason, explain with details.)
Step 2: CROSS OUT (Reread your reasons and details. Cross out any that you decide not to include.)
Step 3: CONNECT (Connect any details that could go into one sentence.)
Step 4: NUMBER (Number the reasons in a logical order.)
Step 5: WRITE (Write your response.)
Step 6: EDIT (Revise and proofread your response.)

Prompt: Pretend that you are trying to convince an alien to become an American citizen. What reasons would you use to support that position?

Planning Box
(position)
(reason)
(explain)
(reason)
(explain)
(reason)
(explain)

Directions: Write your extended response on a separate piece of paper.

Rubric— Extended Response	Student or Partner Rating		Teacher Rating	
1. Did the author tell his/her position in the first sentence?	Yes	Fix up	Yes	No
2. Did the author include at least three **strong, logical** reasons for his/her position?	Yes	Fix up	Yes	No
3. Did the author provide a **strong, logical** explanation for each of his/her reasons?	Yes	Fix up	Yes	No
4. Is the response easy to understand?	Yes	Fix up	Yes	No
5. Did the author correctly spell words, particularly the words found in the article?	Yes	Fix up	Yes	No
6. Did the author use correct capitalization, capitalizing the first word in the sentence and proper names of people, places, and things?	Yes	Fix up	Yes	No
7. Did the author use correct punctuation, including a period at the end of each sentence?	Yes	Fix up	Yes	No

WRITING

Points

(**ACTIVITY A**) *Vocabulary*

List 1: Tell

1. **ratify**   *v.* ▶ (to approve)
2. **relieve**   *v.* ▶ (to reduce or lighten pain, anxiety, etc.)
3. **migrant**   *n.* ▶ (a person who moves from one region to another)
4. **refugees**   *n.* ▶ (people who leave their homes because of danger)
5. **weary**   *adj.* ▶ (tired; worn out)
6. **drought**   *n.* ▶ (a long period of dry weather; lack of rain)

List 2: Strategy Practice

1. **according to**   *adj.* ▶ (as stated in a document)
2. **international**   *adj.* ▶ (concerning two or more countries)
3. **security**   *n.* ▶ (protection from danger)
4. **centralize**   *v.* ▶ (to organize under one point of control)
5. **inception**   *n.* ▶ (beginning)
6. **dispute**   *n.* ▶ (a fight or an argument)
7. **economic**   *adj.* ▶ (having to do with money)
8. **impoverish**   *v.* ▶ (to make very poor)
9. **environmental**   *adj.* ▶ (having to do with the environment)
10. **sustainable**   *adj.* ▶ (able to keep up or maintain over time)

TALLY   VOCABULARY   5

Points

List 3: Word Families

Family 1	**organize**	*v.*	▶ (to provide a structure; to arrange in an orderly way)
	organizing	*v.*	
	organization	*n.*	

Family 2	**moderate**	*v.*	▶ (to preside over something, such as a meeting; to referee)
	moderated	*v.*	
	moderation	*n.*	

Family 3	**diplomacy**	*n.*	▶ (the conducting of relations between or among nations; two or more countries talking to each other)
	diplomatic	*adj.*	
	diplomatically	*adv.*	

Family 4	**universe**	*n.*	▶ (all that exists)
	universal	*adj.*	
	universally	*adv.*	

Family 5	**observe**	*v.*	▶ (to watch closely)
	observation	*n.*	
	observational	*adj.*	

(ACTIVITY B) *Spelling Dictation*

1.	4.
2.	5.
3.	6.

SPELLING 6 *Points*

ACTIVITY C *Background Knowledge*

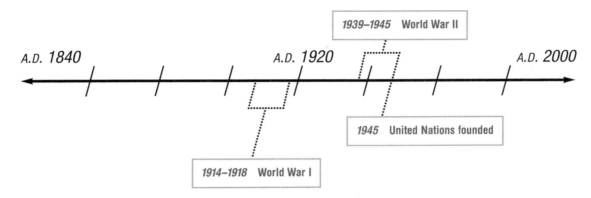

1939–1945   World War II

A.D. *1840*   A.D. *1920*   A.D. *2000*

1945   United Nations founded

1914–1918   World War I

This article will describe why several nations came together in 1945 to create the United Nations. World War I (1914–1918) left much devastation in its wake, and many countries were horrified. Sixty-three countries (but not the United States) decided to become members of the League of Nations in order to work for peace. However, the League of Nations was unwilling to oppose the actions of Germany, Italy, and Japan in the 1930s and ultimately failed to prevent another world war. So, after World War II (1939–1945), the United States hosted a meeting for delegates from 50 countries, who created and agreed to a common set of rules to promote world peace and encourage cooperation.

The Flag of the United Nations

ACTIVITY D *Passage Reading and Comprehension*

The United Nations

By 1945, the world was weary of war. The world had fought World War I and
16 World War II, and many of the world's nations were intent on creating lasting
30 peace. On October 24, 1945, the United Nations was established to do that. (#1)

43 **The Charter**
45 The governing document of the U.N. is its charter. The charter has been
58 ratified, or approved, by all member nations. It describes the roles each member
71 must fulfill. According to the charter, the United Nations has many purposes.
83 One goal is to maintain international peace and security. It also tries to create
97 good relationships among nations and helps them to work with one another to
110 solve international problems. In addition, the U.N. strives to support and
121 improve human rights and basic freedoms. It acts as a centralizing organization
133 for nations that are working toward these goals. (#2)

141 **International Peace and Security**
145 Since its inception, the United Nations has played a major role in trying to
159 create and maintain peace throughout the world. The U.N. can moderate, or
171 referee, disputes among nations. It encourages the nations to resolve conflict
182 through diplomacy rather than war. The U.N. also moderates civil disputes, or
194 disagreements, among groups within one country. It helps a country to resolve
206 problems among its different groups in order to avoid civil war. When armed
219 conflict does occur, the U.N. can send in peacekeeping forces to help decrease
232 tensions. The U.N. can also help rebuild peaceful social, economic, and
243 government systems after a war is over. The United Nations even has a group
257 devoted to trying to make sure that outer space remains peaceful. (#3)

268 **Economic and Social Development**
272 There is a lot of news about the U.N.'s efforts at peacemaking and security,
286 but most of the work the United Nations does is in economic and social
300 development. It works in many parts of the world to relieve poverty.
312 Impoverished countries receive loans, food aid, medical help, and other forms of
324 assistance. The United Nations also addresses global issues that have economic
335 and social impact, such as drug trafficking, AIDS, and environmental problems.
346 It provides protection and help for refugees of countries engaged in armed

358	conflict. The U.N. also provides disaster relief for victims of major natural
370	disasters, such as earthquakes, floods, droughts, and storms. In developing
380	countries, the U.N. also helps disaster-prone areas—those areas consistently
391	affected by such things as hurricanes, earthquakes, and volcanic eruptions—
401	design preparation plans. These plans lessen the impact of a natural disaster. (#4)

Human Rights

413	
415	In 1948, the United Nations adopted a Universal Declaration of Human
426	Rights. This document created an international standard for human rights for all
438	countries to uphold. Since then, the declaration has expanded. It now includes
450	more specific rights for women, minorities, children, migrant workers, and the
461	disabled. All of these human rights are protected by international law. When a
474	country is accused of not upholding these rights, the U.N. sends in an
487	observational team to find out what is happening. (#5)

International Law

495	
497	The United Nations works very hard to develop treaties and agreements that
509	promote peace, security, and sustainable development. When a country signs a
520	United Nations agreement, it becomes part of their law. There are international
532	laws about how to use international waters and air. The U.N. has also created
546	laws to reduce environmental problems, to promote human rights, and to deal
558	with international crime, such as terrorism. These international standards
567	provide a basis for cooperation among many different nations. (#6)

Building Peace

576	
578	Although not all nations cooperate with the United Nations, it is becoming
590	an increasingly powerful voice for peace in the world. The U.N. helps people
603	with basic needs, such as food, medicine, and human rights. But it also helps
617	countries resolve disputes, create agreements, and become friendlier with one
627	another. The United Nations stands apart from the world, trying to make sure its
641	citizens work together in the best ways possible. (#7)
649	

(ACTIVITY E) *Fluency Building*

Cold Timing [ ]　　**Practice 1** [ ]

Practice 2 [ ]　　**Hot Timing** [ ]

(ACTIVITY F) *Comprehension Questions— Multiple Choice and Short Answer*

Comprehension Strategy—Multiple Choice

Step 1: Read the item.

Step 2: Read all of the choices.

Step 3: Think about why each choice might be correct or incorrect. Check the article as needed.

Step 4: From the possible correct choices, select the best answer.

1. (Vocabulary) **Read these sentences from the article: "By 1945, the world was** *weary* **of war. The world had fought World War I and World War II, and many of the world's nations were intent on creating lasting peace." Based on how those sentences read, what does the word** *weary* **mean?**

   a. desirous

   b. extremely tired

   c. resentful

   d. afraid

2. (Compare and Contrast) **How were the League of Nations and the United Nations the same?**

   a. The same countries were members.

   b. Their main purpose was the same: promoting world peace.

   c. They had the same founders.

   d. Their ideas for preventing another world war were the same.

3. (Main Idea) **If the article needed a new title, which would be best?**

   a. *The League of Nations and the United Nations*

   b. *International Support of the United Nations*

   c. *The U.N. as a Peacekeeper*

   d. *The Many Purposes of the United Nations*

4. (Vocabulary) **In the term** *United Nations, United* **means:**

   a. joined together to form one government.

   b. joined together to protect the rights of poor countries.

   c. joined together for a common purpose.

   d. joined together to protect against enemies.

MULTIPLE CHOICE COMPREHENSION

4

Points

Comprehension Strategy—Short Answer

Step 1: Read the item.
Step 2: Turn the question into part of the answer and write it down.
Step 3: Think of the answer or locate the answer in the article.
Step 4: Complete your answer.

1. **Name three issues the United Nations addressed through the creation of international laws.**

   _____

   _____

   _____

   _____

2. **How might the U.N. be able to help a very poor country?**

   _____

   _____

   _____

   _____

SHORT ANSWER COMPREHENSION 4

Points

(ACTIVITY G) *Expository Writing—Summary*

Writing Strategy—Summary

Step 1: LIST (List the details that are important enough to include in the summary.)
Step 2: CROSS OUT (Reread the details. Cross out any that you decide not to include.)
Step 3: CONNECT (Connect any details that could go into one sentence.)
Step 4: NUMBER (Number the details in a logical order.)
Step 5: WRITE (Write your summary.)
Step 6: EDIT (Revise and proofread your summary.)

Prompt: Write a summary of the information contained in *The United Nations* article.

Planning Box
(topic)
(detail)
(detail)
(detail)
(detail)
(detail)
(detail)
(detail)
(detail)
(detail)
(detail)

Directions: Write your summary on a separate piece of paper.

Rubric—Summary	Student or Partner Rating		Teacher Rating	
1. Did the author state the topic and the main idea in the first sentence?	Yes	Fix up	Yes	No
2. Did the author focus on important details?	Yes	Fix up	Yes	No
3. Did the author combine details in some of the sentences?	Yes	Fix up	Yes	No
4. Is the summary easy to understand?	Yes	Fix up	Yes	No
5. Did the author correctly spell words, particularly the words found in the article?	Yes	Fix up	Yes	No
6. Did the author use correct capitalization, capitalizing the first word in the sentence and proper names of people, places, and things?	Yes	Fix up	Yes	No
7. Did the author use correct punctuation, including a period at the end of each sentence?	Yes	Fix up	Yes	No

WRITING

Points

(**ACTIVITY A**) *Vocabulary*

List 1: Tell

1.	barrier	*n.*	▶ (something that blocks the way)
2.	elite	*n.*	▶ (a part of a group regarded as the finest, best, or most powerful)
3.	neutral	*adj.*	▶ (not belonging to any specific group)
4.	pamphlet	*n.*	▶ (a short book with a paper cover)
5.	brochure	*n.*	▶ (a small pamphlet)
6.	pseudonym	*n.*	▶ (a fake name)
7.	Esperanto	*n.*	▶ (an international language created by Lazar Zamenhof)
8.	Esperantists	*n.*	▶ (people who speak Esperanto)

List 2: Strategy Practice

1.	different	*adj.*	▶ (not the same as; unlike one another)
2.	education	*n.*	▶ (the process of gaining knowledge or skill, especially by schooling)
3.	conversation	*n.*	▶ (talk between or among people)
4.	particular	*adj.*	▶ (belonging to a specific group)
5.	affiliate	*v.*	▶ (to join together; unite)
6.	construct	*v.*	▶ (to make or build)
7.	experience	*n.*	▶ (something that a person has done)
8.	necessity	*n.*	▶ (something that is needed)
9.	universal	*adj.*	▶ (shared by all)
10.	actively	*adv.*	▶ (full of action)

TALLY [ ]   VOCABULARY [ ] **5**
Points

List 3: Word Families

Family 1	receive	v.	▶ (to get)
	recipient	n.	
	receptive	adj.	

Family 2	distribute	v.	▶ (to divide and give out in shares)
	distribution	n.	
	distributive	adj.	

Family 3	communicate	v.	▶ (to share thoughts or feelings)
	communication	n.	
	communicator	n.	

Family 4	complicate	v.	▶ (to make difficult or hard to understand)
	complicated	adj.	
	complication	n.	

Family 5	grammar	n.	▶ (rules of a language)
	grammatical	adj.	
	grammatically	adv.	

ACTIVITY B *Spelling Dictation*

1.	4.
2.	5.
3.	6.

SPELLING 6
Points

(ACTIVITY C) *Background Knowledge*

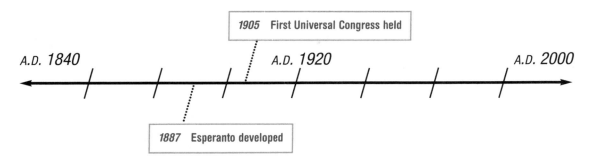

In this article, you will read about Esperanto, which was first proposed in 1887. Esperanto is a constructed language, which is a language that has been invented by a person, rather than evolving over time. Languages such as English, French, and Japanese developed over thousands of years of use. But Esperanto and other constructed languages have been deliberately created. Here is an example of a sentence from the *Wizard of Oz*, written first in English and then in Esperanto, so you can see what it looks like.

Dorothy lived in the midst of the great Kansas prairies, with Uncle Henry, who was a farmer, and Aunt Em, who was the farmer's wife.

Doroteo logxis en la mezo de la granda kamparo de Kansas, kun Onklo Henriko, kiu estis kultivisto, kaj Onklino Em, kiu estis la edzino de la kultivisto.

ACTIVITY D *Passage Reading and Comprehension*

An International Language

	In today's world, it is easier than ever to experience different cultures. People
13	can fly on airplanes to distant countries. They can exchange e-mail with people
26	all over the world. Communication happens at the speed of light. But one barrier
40	still remains to this idea of a global village—the language barrier. Someone who
54	speaks Russian is unable to communicate with someone who speaks Italian. A
66	traveler from Brazil cannot carry on a simple conversation in India. (#1)
77	Although English is often considered an international language, it really is
88	not. English is a complicated, difficult language to learn. It requires many years
101	of study for, say, a Chinese person to grasp the basics of English. Only the elite,
117	well-educated members of society would have enough education to
127	communicate effectively in English if it is not their first language. (#2)

138	**A Dream of Understanding**
142	In the 1860s and 1870s, a boy named Lazar Zamenhof was growing up in the
157	Russian Empire. All around him, he saw people who could not communicate
169	with each other. People in the Russian Empire spoke Russian, German,
180	Hebrew, and Polish. Their language differences kept them separated. (#3)
189	Lazar dreamed that if one language could be created that all people could
202	easily learn and understand, then it would help the world become more
214	peaceful. It would be a neutral language—one that did not belong to any group
229	in particular, but to all of mankind. Lazar was very talented at languages and
243	learned Greek, Latin, German, Russian, French, and English. When he was 15,
255	he decided to begin work on his dream language. (#4)

264	**The Birth of Esperanto**
268	In 1887, Lazar published a pamphlet under the pseudonym Dr. Esperanto.
279	The pamphlet, or brochure, described the necessity of an international
289	language. It explained the simple grammatical rules and provided about 900
300	vocabulary words. It also showed several written examples of the language.
311	People called it "Dr. Esperanto's International Language." Later, they shortened
321	it to just "Esperanto." (#5)
325	People began to distribute the brochure to others. Recipients of the
336	brochure wrote letters to Zamenhof, expressing interest and support for the new
348	language. Some of the letters were even written in the new language! By 1905,

| 362 | the support for Esperanto was so great that a Universal Congress was held. |
| 375 | People came from 20 different countries to explore this new idea. (#6) |

Why Does It Work?

386	
390	Esperanto is an effective international language for several reasons. First of
401	all, it is easy to learn. An average person can master the language in a year or so.
419	Second, it is a neutral language. It is not affiliated with any political or social
434	group. It is everyone's language. (#7)

Esperanto Is Growing

439	
442	Esperanto has not yet become as widespread as Zamenhof hoped. But there
454	are still groups of people who actively promote its use. Around the world, the
468	number of people who use it continues to grow. It is especially popular in central
483	and eastern Europe, eastern Asia (especially mainland China), and some areas of
495	South America. People publish original works of literature and Web pages in
507	Esperanto. Some of the world's radio stations broadcast in Esperanto. Each year,
519	the Universal Congress is held in a different country for Esperantists. Even the
532	United Nations has recognized Esperanto's usefulness and potential. Although
541	Zamenhof's dream was not realized as quickly as he thought it might be, there
555	are many people dedicated to making sure that Esperanto continues to grow. (#8)
567	

(ACTIVITY E) *Fluency Building*

Cold Timing [ ]   **Practice 1** [ ]

Practice 2 [ ]   **Hot Timing** [ ]

ACTIVITY F *Comprehension Questions—*
Multiple Choice and Short Answer

Comprehension Strategy—Multiple Choice

Step 1: Read the item.
Step 2: Read all of the choices.
Step 3: Think about why each choice might be correct or incorrect. Check the article as needed.
Step 4: From the possible correct choices, select the best answer.

1. (Vocabulary) **Read this sentence from the article: "Only the elite, well-educated members of society would have enough education to communicate *effectively* in English if it is not their first language." What does the word *effectively* mean in that sentence?**
   a. loudly
   b. universally
   c. quickly
   d. well

2. (Main Idea) **The main reason that Lazar Zamenhof created Esperanto was:**
   a. because English is a complicated, difficult language to learn.
   b. to allow people of different cultures to communicate with each other.
   c. to bring together Russian, German, Hebrew, and Polish people.
   d. to allow international radio broadcasts.

3. (Cause and Effect) **Why was a *neutral* language created?**
   a. So that it did not belong to one specific group.
   b. So that it would be new.
   c. So that it would be accepted by English, Russian, and Spanish broadcasters.
   d. So that it would be easy to learn.

4. (Compare and Contrast) **Which of these statements about Esperanto and English is *not* true?**
   a. Both are used in many countries.
   b. Both are official languages of many countries.
   c. Both are used for oral and written communication.
   d. Both can be heard on the radio.

MULTIPLE CHOICE COMPREHENSION   4

Comprehension Strategy—Short Answer

Step 1: Read the item.
Step 2: Turn the question into part of the answer and write it down.
Step 3: Think of the answer or locate the answer in the article.
Step 4: Complete your answer.

1. Why is Esperanto considered a *constructed* language?

_____

_____

_____

_____

2. Why did Lazar Zamenhof want to develop a new language?

_____

_____

_____

_____

SHORT ANSWER COMPREHENSION
Points

(ACTIVITY G) *Expository Writing—Extended Response*

Writing Strategy—Extended Response

Step 1: LIST (List the reasons for your position. For each reason, explain with details.)
Step 2: CROSS OUT (Reread your reasons and details. Cross out any that you decide not to include.)
Step 3: CONNECT (Connect any details that could go into one sentence.)
Step 4: NUMBER (Number the reasons in a logical order.)
Step 5: WRITE (Write your response.)
Step 6: EDIT (Revise and proofread your response.)

Prompt: Tell why Esperanto would make a good international language.

Planning Box
(position)
(reason)
(explain)
(reason)
(explain)
(reason)
(explain)
(reason)
(explain)

Directions: Write your extended response on a separate piece of paper.

Rubric— Extended Response	Student or Partner Rating		Teacher Rating	
1. Did the author tell his/her position in the first sentence?	Yes	Fix up	Yes	No
2. Did the author include at least three **strong, logical** reasons for his/her position?	Yes	Fix up	Yes	No
3. Did the author provide a **strong, logical** explanation for each of his/her reasons?	Yes	Fix up	Yes	No
4. Is the response easy to understand?	Yes	Fix up	Yes	No
5. Did the author correctly spell words, particularly the words found in the article?	Yes	Fix up	Yes	No
6. Did the author use correct capitalization, capitalizing the first word in the sentence and proper names of people, places, and things?	Yes	Fix up	Yes	No
7. Did the author use correct punctuation, including a period at the end of each sentence?	Yes	Fix up	Yes	No

WRITING **7**

Points

(ACTIVITY A) *Vocabulary*

List 1: Tell

1. **kanji**   *n.* ▶ (Chinese characters made from lines and brush strokes)

2. **Korea**   *n.* ▶ (a country in Asia)

3. **Taiwan**   *n.* ▶ (an island close to China)

4. **Roman**   *adj.* ▶ (of Rome)

5. **Qin Dynasty**   *n.* ▶ (rulers from the Qin family)

6. **scholars**   *n.* ▶ (learned people; people who spend quite a bit of time studying and learning)

7. **characters**   *n.* ▶ (drawings or pictures)

List 2: Strategy Practice

1. **historians**   *n.* ▶ (people who study the past)

2. **divination**   *n.* ▶ (a type of fortune-telling)

3. **eventually**   *adv.* ▶ (finally; in the end)

4. **informal**   *adj.* ▶ (made for everyday use)

5. **represent**   *v.* ▶ (to look like)

6. **pronunciation**   *n.* ▶ (how something is said)

7. **standardize**   *v.* ▶ (to make the same or uniform)

8. **normalize**   *v.* ▶ (to make normal)

9. **mandatory**   *adj.* ▶ (must be done)

10. **literate**   *adj.* ▶ (able to read and write)

TALLY   **VOCABULARY** 5

Points   *Student Book: Application Lesson 11*   **103**

List 3: Word Families

Family 1	**interpret**	*v.*	► (to tell the meaning of)
	interpreter	*n.*	
	interpretation	*n.*	
Family 2	**origin**	*n.*	► (the beginning of)
	originate	*v.*	
	original	*adj.*	
Family 3	**simple**	*adj.*	► (easy to understand)
	simplified	*v.*	
	simplification	*n.*	
Family 4	**memory**	*n.*	► (things learned and remembered)
	memorize	*v.*	
	memorization	*n.*	
Family 5	**pronounce**	*v.*	► (to say a word correctly)
	pronounceable	*adj.*	
	pronunciation	*n.*	

(ACTIVITY B) *Spelling Dictation*

1.	4.
2.	5.
3.	6.

SPELLING / **6**
Points

(ACTIVITY C) *Background Knowledge*

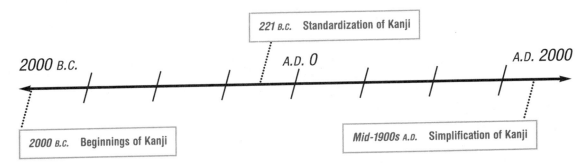

221 B.C. Standardization of Kanji

2000 B.C.

A.D. 0

A.D. 2000

2000 B.C. Beginnings of Kanji

Mid-1900s A.D. Simplification of Kanji

In this article, you will read about the beginnings, or the origins, of the Chinese written language around the year 2000 B.C., approximately 4000 years ago. People in different parts of the world developed different ways of representing their languages. Most alphabets use individual letters or groups of letters to represent sounds. In the Roman alphabet, which is the alphabet used to write English, Spanish, German, Italian, and French, the letters represent sounds and are grouped together to form individual words. In Chinese and Japanese writing, a series of brush strokes form a picture or character that represents a word or concept. Here are some kanji forms and their meanings.

山　　茶　　花
shan　　cha　　hua
mountain　　tea　　flower(s)

Some Examples of Modern Chinese Kanji

ACTIVITY D *Passage Reading and Comprehension*

Kanji

	Have you ever seen Chinese or Japanese writing? Its brush strokes and lines
13	look very different from the Roman alphabet (which uses letters like A, B, C,
27	etc.). This system of writing, used in Japan, Korea, Taiwan, and China, is known
41	as *kanji*. (#1)

The Origin of Kanji

43	
47	Historians believe that kanji originated in China around 2000 B.C. At that
59	time, kings and other leaders would use *divination* in order to answer difficult
72	questions. Divination is like fortune-telling. These leaders interpreted the cracks
83	in bones and turtle shells to mean certain things. Generally, the meaning that
96	was given to a certain set of cracks was determined by the way the cracks
111	looked. In other words, if the cracks sort of looked like a bird, then they would
127	be interpreted to mean "bird." A scribe, an official writer, recorded these
139	interpretations for the king. He made a drawing of the crack and then a drawing
154	of the object it represented. (#2)
159	Eventually, some of these drawings began to be very familiar, as they appeared
172	over and over again. As they appeared more frequently, they were given an
185	informal definition and pronunciation, and the drawing became a character. It is
197	believed that there were about 3000 characters during this early period. Only half
210	of those characters can be understood today. With time, more and more scholars
223	came to view these characters as a sort of writing system. They used this writing
238	system as a way to interpret language through pictures and symbols. But it wasn't
252	until about 221 B.C. that the system began to be standardized. (#3)

The Standardization of Kanji

263	
267	The rulers of the Qin Dynasty decided that most things in China should be
281	normalized. They made roads all the same width and standardized weight and
293	distance measurements. They also created a set of official written characters.
304	The official index contained about 3300 characters, which were mandatory for
315	scholars to learn. (#4)

Kanji Expands

318	
320	Shortly after its standardization, kanji was introduced to Japan. The Japanese
331	adopted kanji as the written expression of their language. Before this, their

343	language was only spoken. During the next thousand years, kanji rapidly
354	expanded and changed. China was developing new technologies, ideas, and
364	concepts. Therefore, new words and characters were invented to express these
375	ideas. The number of characters the Chinese were using increased to about
387	30,000. (#5)

388	**Modern Kanji**
390	During the 20th century, both China and Japan simplified their kanji. Before
402	World War II, a person had to know more than 12,000 characters to be able to
418	read the newspaper. That is a lot of characters to memorize! Because kanji was
432	so difficult to learn, less than half the population of each country was able to
447	read. The governments of the two countries decided to simplify the characters.
459	However, they simplified the same characters in different ways. As a result, the
472	two written languages appear very different now. (#6)
479	Each country also determined a set of basic kanji for everyday life. There are
493	about 100,000 kanji in existence, but many of them are no longer used. Even the
508	most highly educated students may know only between 7,000 and 12,000
519	characters. In Japan, recognition of about 2,000 kanji is necessary to read
531	newspapers; in China, recognition of 4,000–8,000 kanji is necessary. Because of
543	the simplification of kanji, many more people are now literate in China and
556	Japan. Although it is still difficult to learn, kanji continues to be an important
570	part of Chinese and Japanese cultures. (#7)
576	

(ACTIVITY E) *Fluency Building*

Cold Timing [　　　]

Practice 1 [　　　]

Practice 2 [　　　]

Hot Timing [　　　]

(ACTIVITY F) *Comprehension Questions— Multiple Choice and Short Answer*

Comprehension Strategy—Multiple Choice

Step 1: Read the item.

Step 2: Read all of the choices.

Step 3: Think about why each choice might be correct or incorrect. Check the article as needed.

Step 4: From the possible correct choices, select the best answer.

1. (Vocabulary) **What does the heading "The *Standardization* of Kanji" mean?**
   a. The characters were made the same size.
   b. A set of official characters was selected in each country.
   c. The same characters were used in Japan, China, and Korea.
   d. The same number of characters was chosen in each country of Asia.

2. (Compare and Contrast) **What is the *major* difference between the Roman alphabet and kanji?**
   a. The Roman alphabet was developed in Europe, while kanji was developed in Asia.
   b. Kanji has been standardized recently, while the Roman alphabet was standardized many centuries ago.
   c. The Roman alphabet is used in many European countries, such as Spain and France, while kanji is used in China and Japan.
   d. The Roman alphabet letters represent sounds, while kanji characters represent words or concepts.

3. (Cause and Effect) **China and Japan simplified their kanji:**
   a. so that the two languages would look different.
   b. to make the drawings more attractive.
   c. to allow more people to become literate.
   d. to save time and paper.

4. (Main Idea) **Which sentence gives the best summary of this article?**
   a. Kanji characters look very different than the letters of the Roman alphabet used to represent English.
   b. Kanji, a system of writing that represents words with characters, was developed in Asia and has changed over time.
   c. Standardization of kanji led to an official set of characters that students could learn.
   d. To make kanji available to more people, it was simplified in China and Japan.

MULTIPLE CHOICE COMPREHENSION

Points

Comprehension Strategy—Short Answer

Step 1: Read the item.
Step 2: Turn the question into part of the answer and write it down.
Step 3: Think of the answer or locate the answer in the article.
Step 4: Complete your answer.

1. How is kanji different from the Roman alphabet (e.g., A, B, C)?

_____

_____

_____

_____

2. Why is kanji difficult to learn?

_____

_____

_____

_____

SHORT ANSWER COMPREHENSION

Points

(ACTIVITY G) *Expository Writing—Summary*

Writing Strategy—Summary

Step 1: LIST (List the details that are important enough to include in the summary.)
Step 2: CROSS OUT (Reread the details. Cross out any that you decide not to include.)
Step 3: CONNECT (Connect any details that could go into one sentence.)
Step 4: NUMBER (Number the details in a logical order.)
Step 5: WRITE (Write your summary.)
Step 6: EDIT (Revise and proofread your summary.)

Prompt: Write a summary of the information on kanji presented in this article.

Planning Box	
(topic)	
(detail)	
(detail)	
(detail)	
(detail)	
(detail)	
(detail)	
(detail)	
(detail)	

Directions: Write your summary on a separate piece of paper.

Rubric—Summary	Student or Partner Rating	Teacher Rating
1. Did the author state the topic and the main idea in the first sentence?	Yes Fix up	Yes No
2. Did the author focus on important details?	Yes Fix up	Yes No
3. Did the author combine details in some of the sentences?	Yes Fix up	Yes No
4. Is the summary easy to understand?	Yes Fix up	Yes No
5. Did the author correctly spell words, particularly the words found in the article?	Yes Fix up	Yes No
6. Did the author use correct capitalization, capitalizing the first word in the sentence and proper names of people, places, and things?	Yes Fix up	Yes No
7. Did the author use correct punctuation, including a period at the end of each sentence?	Yes Fix up	Yes No

WRITING **7**

Points

ACTIVITY A *Vocabulary*

List 1: Tell

1.	Mozambique	*n.*	▶ (an island country off the coast of Africa)
2.	continent	*n.*	▶ (a large landmass)
3.	Europe	*n.*	▶ (a continent across the Atlantic Ocean)
4.	Asia	*n.*	▶ (the largest continent)
5.	Eurasia	*n.*	▶ (Europe and Asia as one continent)
6.	Kenya	*n.*	▶ (a country in Africa)
7.	sodium carbonate	*n.*	▶ (a chemical for making glass and soap)
8.	Lake Magadi	*n.*	▶ (a lake in Kenya)
9.	Lake Naivasha	*n.*	▶ (a lake in Kenya)

List 2: Strategy Practice

1.	enormous	*adj.*	▶ (very large)
2.	geography	*n.*	▶ (the natural features of a particular place or region)
3.	collision	*n.*	▶ (coming together with force)
4.	economy	*n.*	▶ (the use of money, goods, and services)
5.	concentration	*n.*	▶ (a large amount of a substance gathered in one place, resulting in increased strength or density)
6.	altitude	*n.*	▶ (the height of land)
7.	carnations	*n.*	▶ (a type of flower)
8.	geothermally	*adv.*	▶ (having to do with heat from the earth)
9.	commodity	*n.*	▶ (something that can be bought and sold)
10.	speculate	*v.*	▶ (to predict)

TALLY ☐ 　　VOCABULARY 5

Points

List 3: Word Families

Family 1	geology	n.	▶ (the study of the earth's history and formation)
	geologist	n.	
	geological	adj.	

Family 2	preserve	v.	▶ (to maintain or keep)
	preservation	n.	
	preservationist	n.	

Family 3	vary	v.	▶ (to change or make different)
	variety	n.	
	various	adj.	

Family 4	popular	adj.	▶ (liked by a lot of people)
	populate	v.	
	population	n.	

Family 5	aqua	n.	▶ (water)
	aquarium	n.	
	aquatic	adj.	

ACTIVITY B *Spelling Dictation*

1.	4.
2.	5.
3.	6.

SPELLING 6
Points

ACTIVITY C Background Knowledge

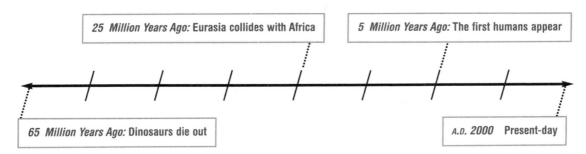

25 Million Years Ago: Eurasia collides with Africa

5 Million Years Ago: The first humans appear

65 Million Years Ago: Dinosaurs die out

A.D. 2000 Present-day

The article you will read today describes Africa's Great Rift Valley. A rift is an opening made by splitting. There are many rifts, or splits, in the earth's surface. The Great Rift Valley is a visible part of the longest rift in the world. You will learn where this very deep valley is located, how it was formed, and its importance to the people of the region.

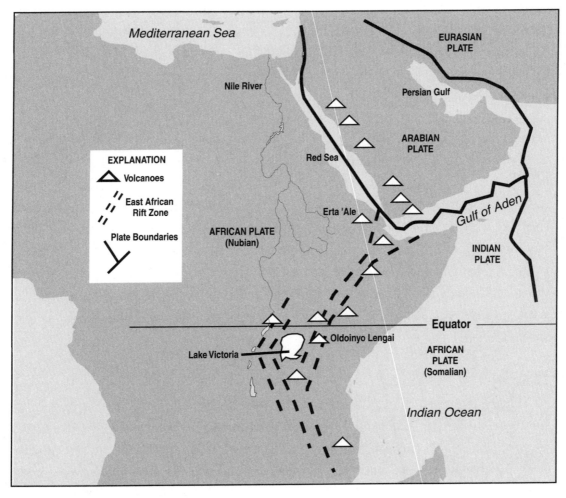

Map of the Great Rift Valley in Africa

ACTIVITY D *Passage Reading and Comprehension*

Africa's Great Rift Valley

	In eastern Africa, a deep valley runs from north to south, framed on either
14	side by grassy plains and enormous mountains. This valley is home to many of
28	the world's deepest lakes. The valley is the visible part of a deep rift in the
44	earth's crust. This area, stretching from northeastern Africa down into
54	Mozambique, is known as the Great Rift Valley. (#1)
62	**How It Was Formed**
66	The continents on the earth did not always look the way they do today. Many
81	millions of years ago, Europe and Asia were one continent. Geologists call that
94	continent Eurasia. Continents drift very slowly, moving around the earth's
104	surface. Perhaps 25 million years ago, Eurasia collided with Africa. This collision
116	created enough force to crack the earth's crust in eastern Africa in two places.
130	As these cracks pulled away from each other, the land dropped, and a valley
144	formed between them. The two cracks are known as the Western Rift and the
158	Eastern Rift. (#2)
160	**Geography of the Valley**
164	Because of the deep cracks in the earth's crust, the Rift Valley has a number
179	of active and inactive volcanoes. These volcanoes give the landscape its
190	mountainous appearance. In addition to the volcanoes, there are many lakes in
202	the Rift Valley. The Western Rift has some of the deepest lakes in the world.
217	Because the lakes are isolated, and the water does not flow anywhere, they can
231	be home to fish and aquatic life that cannot be found anywhere else in the
246	world. Many of the Rift Valley's lakes have high concentrations of minerals. In
259	some places, the lakes are rich in soda, which can be mined and sold as a raw
276	material. (#3)
277	**Climate**
278	There is a variety of climates in the Great Rift Valley. They vary greatly
292	because the altitude changes throughout the region. Generally, as the altitude
303	grows higher, the temperatures drop. Lower lands tend to be hotter and drier.
316	Around the shores of some of the lakes as well as on the coast, however, it is hot
334	and humid, with a high rainfall. (#4)

340	**Plant and Animal Life**
344	Because there is such a variety of climates in the Great Rift Valley, it
358	supports a staggering variety of plant and animal life. In the valley itself, you
372	might find lions, elephants, leopards, zebras, and large birds of prey. Many of
385	the lakes contain rare and unusual varieties of fish and aquatic plants, most of
399	which do not exist anywhere else. Flamingos, pelicans, storks, and other fish-
411	eating birds populate the shorelines. In some areas of the Great Rift Valley,
424	national parks have been created to protect and preserve the numerous
435	creatures and plants that are native to this amazing region. (#5)
445	**Resources**
446	The people who live in the various regions of the Great Rift Valley have
460	discovered a number of resources that help drive their economies. In Kenya,
472	they export the sodium carbonate from Lake Magadi. This is used as a raw
486	material in making things such as soap and glass. The climate and rich soil near
501	Lake Naivasha allow farmers to grow a popular flower, the carnation, which is
514	then shipped to Europe for sale. The steam and heat that rise from the volcanic
529	regions are harnessed geothermally, resulting in electricity. In addition,
538	geologists predict that there may be sizeable quantities of oil in the Great Rift
552	Valley. Fish from the various lakes provide food for local people as well as a
567	commodity that can be sold. Finally, the vegetation, climate, and wildlife of such
580	places as Kenya and Tanzania have created an increasingly popular tourist
591	industry. (#6)
592	**The Rift Continues**
595	Amazingly, the valley is slowly widening as the rifts grow larger. Some
607	geologists speculate that in millions of years, the eastern part of Africa may
620	detach, forming a separate landmass. Although the changes happen slowly, the
631	volcanoes, shifting rock, and human impact will continue to shape this unique
643	and interesting region of the world. (#7)
649	

(ACTIVITY E) *Fluency Building*

Cold Timing		**Practice 1**	
Practice 2		**Hot Timing**	

(ACTIVITY F) *Comprehension Questions—*
Multiple Choice and Short Answer

Comprehension Strategy—Multiple Choice

Step 1: Read the item.
Step 2: Read all of the choices.
Step 3: Think about why each choice might be correct or incorrect. Check the article as needed.
Step 4: From the possible correct choices, select the best answer.

1. (Vocabulary) **Read this sentence from the passage: "In eastern Africa, a deep valley runs from north to south, *framed* on either side by grassy plains and enormous mountains." What does *framed* mean in that sentence?**
   a. surrounded
   b. pictured
   c. visible
   d. mapped

2. (Cause and Effect) **The Great Rift Valley has a variety of altitudes (heights of land). As a *result*, the following is true:**
   a. Fish from the various lakes can be used as food.
   b. There is a variety of climates in the Great Rift Valley.
   c. Tourism has gradually expanded.
   d. The lakes contain high concentrations of minerals.

3. (Cause and Effect) **There is a huge variety of plants and animals in the Great Rift Valley because:**
   a. there are active and inactive volcanoes in the area.
   b. the plants and animals came from Eurasia and Africa when the continents collided.
   c. the minerals in the soil support the growth of plants and the animals that eat those plants.
   d. there is a variety of climates in the Great Rift Valley.

4. (Cause and Effect) **Many of the fish in the Great Rift Valley lakes are found only there because:**
   a. the fish can live only in the mineral-rich lakes of the Great Rift Valley.
   b. the fish live in lakes that don't flow into other rivers, lakes, or oceans.
   c. the fish can eat only the plants in the lakes.
   d. the fish cannot swim far enough to enter a different lake.

MULTIPLE CHOICE COMPREHENSION

Points

Comprehension Strategy—Short Answer

Step 1: Read the item.
Step 2: Turn the question into part of the answer and write it down.
Step 3: Think of the answer or locate the answer in the article.
Step 4: Complete your answer.

1. **Name some of the resources of the Great Rift Valley.**

_____

_____

_____

_____

2. **What do some geologists think will happen in eastern Africa in a million years?**

_____

_____

_____

_____

SHORT ANSWER COMPREHENSION 4

Points

(ACTIVITY G) *Expository Writing—Summary*

Writing Strategy—Summary

Step 1: LIST (List the details that are important enough to include in the summary.)
Step 2: CROSS OUT (Reread the details. Cross out any that you decide not to include.)
Step 3: CONNECT (Connect any details that could go into one sentence.)
Step 4: NUMBER (Number the details in a logical order.)
Step 5: WRITE (Write your summary.)
Step 6: EDIT (Revise and proofread your summary.)

Prompt: Write a summary of the information about the Great Rift Valley.

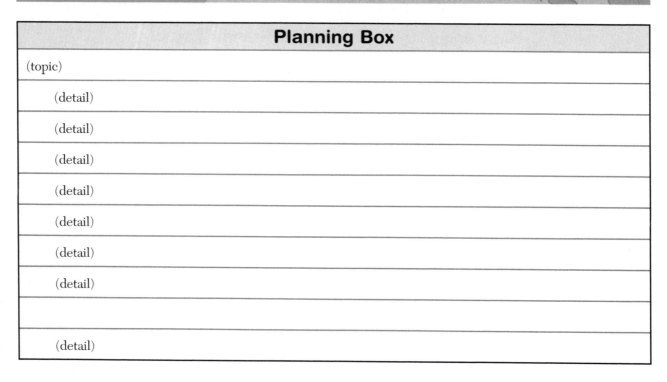

Planning Box

(topic)
(detail)
(detail)
(detail)
(detail)
(detail)
(detail)
(detail)
(detail)

Directions: Write your summary on a separate piece of paper.

Rubric— Summary	Student or Partner Rating		Teacher Rating	
1. Did the author state the topic and the main idea in the first sentence?	Yes	Fix up	Yes	No
2. Did the author focus on important details?	Yes	Fix up	Yes	No
3. Did the author combine details in some of the sentences?	Yes	Fix up	Yes	No
4. Is the summary easy to understand?	Yes	Fix up	Yes	No
5. Did the author correctly spell words, particularly the words found in the article?	Yes	Fix up	Yes	No
6. Did the author use correct capitalization, capitalizing the first word in the sentence and proper names of people, places, and things?	Yes	Fix up	Yes	No
7. Did the author use correct punctuation, including a period at the end of each sentence?	Yes	Fix up	Yes	No

WRITING 7 *Points*

(ACTIVITY A) *Vocabulary*

List 1: Tell

1. **Nepal**   *n.* ▶ (a small country in eastern Asia)
2. **Mt. Everest**   *n.* ▶ (the highest mountain in the world, located in Nepal)
3. **Sherpas**   *n.* ▶ (people who live in the mountains of Nepal)
4. **Khumbu Valley**   *n.* ▶ (south of Mt. Everest)
5. **Tibet**   *n.* ▶ (a country next to Nepal)
6. **Nangpa La**   *n.* ▶ (a mountain pass between Tibet and Nepal)
7. **Buddhism**   *n.* ▶ (a religion based on the teachings of Buddha)
8. **Nyingmapa Buddhism**   *n.* ▶ (a type of Buddhism)
9. **Tengboche Monastery**   *n.* ▶ (a religious gathering place located on Mt. Everest)
10. **Chomolungma**   *n.* ▶ (the Sherpa name for Mt. Everest)

List 2: Strategy Practice

1. **prowess**   *n.* ▶ (great ability or skill)
2. **expedition**   *n.* ▶ (a trip or journey for a definite purpose)
3. **fertilizer**   *n.* ▶ (something added to the soil to help things grow)
4. **alienate**   *v.* ▶ (to cause to be unfriendly)
5. **occupation**   *n.* ▶ (the seizure and control of a country by military force)
6. **prosperity**   *n.* ▶ (success, wealth)
7. **substantial**   *adj.* ▶ (important)
8. **spirituality**   *n.* ▶ (concern with things of the spirit or soul)
9. **deforestation**   *n.* ▶ (the result of cutting down forests or trees)
10. **heritage**   *n.* ▶ (something passed down through families)

List 3: Word Families

Family 1	**mountain**	*n.*	▶	(land rising to a great height)
	mountainous	*adj.*	▶	
	mountaineers	*n.*	▶	
Family 2	**comprehend**	*v.*	▶	(to understand)
	comprehension	*n.*	▶	
	comprehensible	*adj.*	▶	
Family 3	**prosper**	*v.*	▶	(to have success, wealth)
	prosperous	*adj.*	▶	
	prosperity	*n.*	▶	
Family 4	**industry**	*n.*	▶	(a manufacturing business)
	industrial	*adj.*	▶	
	industrious	*adj.*	▶	
Family 5	**tradition**	*n.*	▶	(a continued pattern of doing something the same way as it was done in the past)
	traditionally	*adv.*	▶	
	traditionalist	*n.*	▶	

(ACTIVITY B) *Spelling Dictation*

1.	**4.**
2.	**5.**
3.	**6.**

SPELLING 6 *Points*

ACTIVITY C *Background Knowledge*

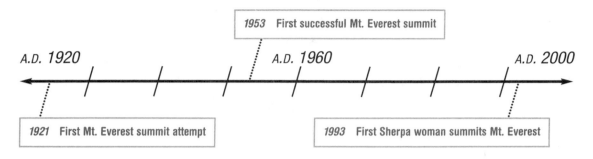

1953 First successful Mt. Everest summit

A.D. *1920*   A.D. *1960*   A.D. *2000*

1921 First Mt. Everest summit attempt

1993 First Sherpa woman summits Mt. Everest

The Sherpas are an ethnic group of people who live in the mountains of Nepal, the highest mountains in the world. Because they live and work in high, mountainous places, Sherpas have adapted to these altitudes, and thus often work as mountaineers for people who climb Mt. Everest. Since the first successful trip up Everest by Sir Edmund Hillary in 1953, Sherpa guides have been traveling with Everest expeditions.

Nima Sherpa photograph courtesy of Linda E. Keyes

Sherpa

(ACTIVITY D) *Passage Reading and Comprehension*

Sherpas

	High in the mountains of Nepal, the Sherpas live in the Khumbu Valley. This
14	valley is considered the southern gateway to Mt. Everest. Sherpas are best
26	known for their climbing prowess and excellent guidance to Everest climbing
37	expeditions. But they have their own culture and customs apart from that as
50	mountain guides. (#1)

52	**Food at 14,000 Feet**
56	Traditionally, Sherpas have made their living through trade and agriculture.
66	They herd yaks, a large shaggy mammal similar to a buffalo. The yak fur
80	provides wool for clothing, the hide provides leather for shoes, and the dung
93	(manure) provides fuel for cooking as well as fertilizer for agriculture. The
105	Sherpas drink the yak's milk. They also make it into butter and cheese. (#2)
118	The Sherpas used to trade with Tibet, across the Nangpa La Pass. They
131	would drive their yak herds across the 19,000-foot pass, carrying buffalo hides
144	and other items. They would return with salt and wool. But trade of goods
158	across the pass has almost completely stopped because of the Chinese
169	occupation of Tibet. (#3)
172	The Sherpas also grow food. Potatoes, which can still grow well at high
185	altitudes, are one of their staples, or basic foods. Potatoes are mixed with meats
199	and vegetables to form a stew. This stew, along with lentils and rice, is their
214	primary meal. Sherpas drink lots of tea, often sweetened with a great deal of
228	sugar and milk. (#4)

231	**Religious Life**
233	The Sherpas practice a sect of Buddhism known as *Nyingmapa* Buddhism.
244	Because of their religious beliefs, the Sherpas have always honored the
255	mountains of their region as the homes of gods and goddesses. For example, the
269	Sherpas believe that Mt. Everest, known as *Chomolungma* in the Tibetan
280	language, is the home of the goddess of humans and prosperity. For centuries,
293	the Sherpas kept the mountains sacred by not climbing them. But the allure of
307	Westerners and their money tempted the Sherpas to accept climbing as part of
320	their culture. For modern religious ceremonies and festivals, the Sherpas often
331	gather at the famous Tengboche Monastery, located 16,000 feet up the north
343	side of Mt. Everest. (#5)

347	**Language**
348	The Sherpas speak a language that is related to modern Tibetan. But the two
362	languages have grown to be more and more different from each other over the
376	years. This makes communication between the two groups very difficult. Only
387	parts of the language are mutually comprehensible. The languages grew apart for
399	two reasons. First, the Sherpa language is not standardized, meaning that the rules
412	of the language are not written down or formally recognized. Second, the Sherpa
425	language does not have a written alphabet. Some people are trying to introduce a
439	written script into the Sherpa language; however, the script would be based on the
453	Tibetan alphabet. Many people feel that the Sherpas would not accept the script
466	because it might not represent the language spoken by the Sherpas (#6)
477	**Mountaineering**
478	In 1921, some Englishmen made the first expedition to climb Mt. Everest.
490	Sherpas were hired to help them. By the 1970s, mountaineering had become a
503	substantial industry for the Sherpas. Many will travel from their villages to the cities,
517	where the foreign climbing expeditions will hire local guides. The Western climbers
529	have influenced the Sherpa culture. Many Sherpa men now wear Western-style
541	clothing. The Sherpa culture and spirituality have influenced the climbers. But not
553	all effects of mountaineering have been positive for the Sherpas. (#7)
563	Western influences, such as deforestation and litter, have become major
573	problems in the Sherpa region. Large numbers of trees have been cut down to
587	make way for new settlements and more agriculture and to be used as fuel in
602	the form of firewood. Everest base camp, the starting point for Everest
614	expeditions, was littered with used oxygen bottles, garbage, and other evidence
625	of the many climbers. However, recent efforts to clean up base camp and lower
639	regions of Everest have succeeded. In 1976, the Khumbu region was declared a
652	national park. The national park staff and other Sherpa groups have also begun
665	to manage the forests and other natural resources. These efforts will help ensure
678	that the Sherpas can continue to maintain their culture and heritage and to
691	preserve their traditions and region. (#8)
696	

(**ACTIVITY E**) *Fluency Building*

Cold Timing		**Practice 1**	
Practice 2		**Hot Timing**	

ACTIVITY F *Comprehension Questions—*
Multiple Choice and Short Answer

Comprehension Strategy—Multiple Choice

Step 1: Read the item.
Step 2: Read all of the choices.
Step 3: Think about why each choice might be correct or incorrect. Check the article as needed.
Step 4: From the possible correct choices, select the best answer.

1. (Vocabulary) **In the article, it states " . . . the *allure* of Westerners and their money led the Sherpas to accept climbing as part of their culture." What does that sentence mean?**

   a. The Sherpas had always climbed mountains, but now they did it for money.

   b. While the Sherpas had not always climbed the mountains, the promise of the Westerners' money made them change their ways.

   c. Up until the arrival of Westerners, climbing was a religious act.

   d. The Sherpas historically have followed Easterners, not Westerners.

2. (Main Idea) **Reread the second paragraph in the article. Which sentence below gives the main idea of the paragraph?**

   a. Yaks provide the Sherpas with food.

   b. Yaks are as important to the Sherpas as cattle are to us.

   c. Yaks meet many of the needs of the Sherpas.

   d. Yaks support agriculture by supplying fertilizer.

3. (Cause and Effect) **Which of the following is *not* a result of Western climbers' interactions with the Sherpas?**

   a. Many Sherpa men now wear Western-style clothing.

   b. Many Sherpa men work away from their villages.

   c. More Sherpa men work as guides for climbing expeditions.

   d. Sherpas no longer have the majority of their survival needs met by yaks.

4. (Main Idea) **If this article needed a new title, which would be best?**

   a. *East Meets West on Mount Everest*

   b. *The Culture of the Sherpas*

   c. *Mount Everest—Home of Gods and Goddesses*

   d. *The Climbers—Western Mountaineers and the Sherpas*

MULTIPLE CHOICE COMPREHENSION

Points

Comprehension Strategy—Short Answer

Step 1: Read the item.
Step 2: Turn the question into part of the answer and write it down.
Step 3: Think of the answer or locate the answer in the article.
Step 4: Complete your answer.

1. What are some ways that yaks are useful to the Sherpas?

_____

_____

_____

_____

2. What are some of the foods eaten by the Sherpas?

_____

_____

_____

_____

SHORT ANSWER COMPREHENSION 4
Points

(ACTIVITY G) *Expository Writing—Extended Response*

Writing Strategy—Extended Response

Step 1: LIST (List the reasons for your position. For each reason, explain with details.)
Step 2: CROSS OUT (Reread your reasons and details. Cross out any that you decide not to include.)
Step 3: CONNECT (Connect any details that could go into one sentence.)
Step 4: NUMBER (Number the reasons in a logical order.)
Step 5: WRITE (Write your response.)
Step 6: EDIT (Revise and proofread your response.)

Prompt: Describe how a Sherpa's life is different from your own.

Planning Box

(position)

   (reason)

      (explain)

   (reason)

      (explain)

   (reason)

      (explain)

   (reason)

      (explain)

Directions: Write your extended response on a separate piece of paper.

Rubric— Extended Response	Student or Partner Rating		Teacher Rating	
1. Did the author tell his/her position in the first sentence?	Yes	Fix up	Yes	No
2. Did the author include at least three **strong, logical** reasons for his/her position?	Yes	Fix up	Yes	No
3. Did the author provide a **strong, logical** explanation for each of his/her reasons?	Yes	Fix up	Yes	No
4. Is the response easy to understand?	Yes	Fix up	Yes	No
5. Did the author correctly spell words, particularly the words found in the article?	Yes	Fix up	Yes	No
6. Did the author use correct capitalization, capitalizing the first word in the sentence and proper names of people, places, and things?	Yes	Fix up	Yes	No
7. Did the author use correct punctuation, including a period at the end of each sentence?	Yes	Fix up	Yes	No

WRITING **7**

Points

ACTIVITY A *Vocabulary*

List 1: Tell

1.	**Rapa Nui**	*n.* ▶	(another name for Easter Island)
2.	**Chile**	*n.* ▶	(a country on the west side of South America)
3.	**intrigue**	*v.* ▶	(to make someone be curious about)
4.	**archaeological**	*adj.* ▶	(having to do with how people lived in the past)
5.	**Polynesian**	*adj.* ▶	(of islands in the Pacific, between Hawaii and New Zealand)
6.	**revere**	*v.* ▶	(to feel deep respect for)
7.	**Peru**	*n.* ▶	(a country north of Chile)
8.	**Incas**	*n.* ▶	(Indian people of Peru)
9.	**Moai**	*n.* ▶	(stone head statues on Easter Island)
10.	**quarry**	*n.* ▶	(a place where stone is cut)

List 2: Strategy Practice

1.	**integrate**	*v.* ▶	(to make whole by bringing parts together)
2.	**overpopulate**	*v.* ▶	(to have too many people living in a certain area)
3.	**conclusion**	*n.* ▶	(a final decision or opinion reached after some thought)
4.	**massive**	*adj.* ▶	(very large)
5.	**elongate**	*v.* ▶	(to make longer)
6.	**inhabitants**	*n.* ▶	(people who live in a place)
7.	**ceremonial**	*adj.* ▶	(related to a ceremony)
8.	**destination**	*n.* ▶	(a place to which a person is going)
9.	**fascinate**	*v.* ▶	(to hold the attention of by being very interesting)
10.	**primitive**	*adj.* ▶	(at an earlier stage of development)

TALLY ☐   VOCABULARY **5**
Points

List 3: Word Families

Family 1	explore	v.	▶ (to travel in order to learn about places)
	explorer	n.	▶
	exploration	n.	▶

Family 2	discover	v.	▶ (to learn about for the first time)
	discoverer	n.	▶
	discovery	n.	▶

Family 3	migrate	v.	▶ (to move from one place to another)
	migration	n.	▶
	immigration	n.	▶

Family 4	navigate	v.	▶ (to steer or direct the course of a ship or aircraft)
	navigator	n.	▶
	navigation	n.	▶

Family 5	explain	v.	▶ (to make clear and understandable)
	explanatory	adj.	▶
	explanation	n.	▶

ACTIVITY B *Spelling Dictation*

1.	4.
2.	5.
3.	6.

SPELLING   6
Points

(ACTIVITY C) *Background Knowledge*

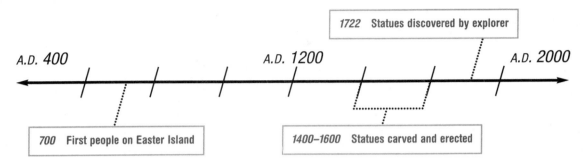

Since ancient times, people have built and erected statues to honor their ancestors and the gods whom they worshipped. The article you will read today describes the discovery of massive stone heads located on a small, isolated island in the Pacific Ocean. These statues were erected about 400 to 600 years ago. They are quite remarkable for their shape, size, and positioning. Interestingly, scientists still cannot explain their significance or their presence on Easter Island.

Easter Island Statues

(ACTIVITY D) *Passage Reading and Comprehension*

Easter Island

15	Easter Island, also known as Rapa Nui, is located west of Chile, in the South Pacific Ocean. It is called Easter Island because the Dutch explorer who
27	discovered the island landed there on Easter Day, 1722. He discovered an
39	isolated island and a group of people who lived there. He also discovered a series
54	of enormous statues. These statues continue to puzzle and intrigue scientists. (#1)

The Early Inhabitants

65

68   Surrounded on all sides by thousands of miles of open ocean, Easter Island
81 has been home to people for more than a thousand years. Archaeological
93 evidence suggests that people have lived there since around A.D. 700. Easter
105 Island legend tells of a Polynesian chief who was the first to come to the island.
121 (The Polynesian people hail, or come, from islands in the Pacific between
133 Hawaii and New Zealand.) He brought his wife and extended family in a double
147 canoe from an unknown island and founded Easter Island culture. (#2)

Island Culture

157

159   Pacific Islanders have always been deeply connected to the ocean. Unlike
170 Europeans, who feared the open seas, islanders revere and respect the water,
182 integrating it into their lives. They traveled from island to island in double
195 canoes. Double canoes were made of island woods and fibers and were used for
209 ocean travel. Early Polynesians were masters of navigation, finding their way
220 from place to place by stars and other natural signs. When small islands became
234 overpopulated, they would set out in their canoes to other islands. This concept
247 may be part of the legend Easter Islanders tell about their origins. (#3)

259   In spite of this legend, scientists have not come to any final conclusions
272 about the origins of the people of Easter Island. Some evidence suggests that
285 people did, in fact, migrate from other Polynesian Islands. But other evidence
297 suggests that the original Easter Island people were Incas who migrated from
309 Peru. Scientists continue to debate the origins of Easter Islanders. But this is
322 not the only puzzle that Easter Island has to offer. (#4)

The Moai

332

334   Along Easter Island's coast stand massive stone heads. They are an average of
347 13 feet high and weigh 14 tons. The islanders call them *Moai*. There are nearly

362	900 of the statues on the island. Each statue stands with its back to the sea.
378	Scientists speculate that they were all carved, moved, and raised between A.D.
390	1400 and 1600. They are all carved in the same style—gigantic heads with
404	elongated ears and noses. Each statue is carved from a soft volcanic rock called
418	*tuff.* The rock was mined from a crater on the island. Explorers found large
432	unfinished statues still in the quarry. (#5)
438	But there is no explanation of how or why they got where they are. How did
454	the people transport and erect such enormous statues? Why did they carve them
467	at all? Some speculate that the heads are likenesses of great leaders. Others
480	suggest that the heads, because of their size, are of ceremonial importance,
492	serving as a connection between the people and their gods. (#6)
502	**Easter Island Today**
505	Today, Easter Island is a popular travel destination. People are attracted to
517	its mystery and its statues. The inhabitants of Easter Island, descendants of the
530	primitive sculptors, run the tourism industry themselves. They celebrate their
540	Polynesian and island heritage through festivals and tours. Archaeologists and
550	other scientists continue to study the Moai, trying to learn the secrets of the
564	giant heads. Fortunately, the entire island has been preserved as a Chilean
576	national park, ensuring that its beauty and wonders will continue to fascinate
588	people for years to come. (#7)
593	

(ACTIVITY E) *Fluency Building*

Cold Timing [ ]   **Practice 1** [ ]

Practice 2 [ ]   **Hot Timing** [ ]

(ACTIVITY F) *Comprehension Questions—*
Multiple Choice and Short Answer

Comprehension Strategy—Multiple Choice

Step 1: Read the item.
Step 2: Read all of the choices.
Step 3: Think about why each choice might be correct or incorrect. Check the article as needed.
Step 4: From the possible correct choices, select the best answer.

1. (Vocabulary) **Read this sentence from the article: "*Archaeologists* and other scientists continue to study the Moai, trying to learn the secrets of the giant heads." What does the word *archaeologists* mean in that sentence?**
   a. People who study past human life as revealed by relics (e.g., dishes, paintings, tools).
   b. Ancient people who lived before a written language was developed.
   c. People who study ancient people by interviewing them.
   d. People who sell art, including paintings and statues.

2. (Cause and Effect) **Scientists are intrigued by the statues on Easter Island because:**
   a. of the legend about the Polynesian chief who brought his family to Easter Island.
   b. the statues are huge and face away from the sea.
   c. the origins of the people on the island remain a mystery.
   d. how and why the statues were built remain a mystery.

3. (Cause and Effect) **What is the main reason that people might visit Easter Island today?**
   a. People love the warm climate and white-sand beaches.
   b. People are very curious about why and how people arrived on Easter Island.
   c. People are very curious about why and how the statues were constructed.
   d. People wish to celebrate Easter on Easter Island.

4. (Main Idea) **If the article needed a new title, which would be best?**
   a. *Easter Island—A New Home to Polynesians*
   b. *Easter Island—Land of Mystery*
   c. *Easter Island—A Holy Destination*
   d. *Easter Island—A Chilean National Park*

MULTIPLE CHOICE COMPREHENSION

4

Points

Comprehension Strategy—Short Answer

Step 1: Read the item.
Step 2: Turn the question into part of the answer and write it down.
Step 3: Think of the answer or locate the answer in the article.
Step 4: Complete your answer.

1. **What do archaeologists think the stone heads might represent?**

_____

_____

_____

_____

2. **Why do you think people might like to travel to Easter Island on vacation?**

_____

_____

_____

_____

SHORT ANSWER COMPREHENSION

Points

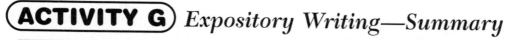

APPLICATION LESSON

14

ACTIVITY G *Expository Writing—Summary*

Writing Strategy—Summary

Step 1: LIST (List the details that are important enough to include in the summary.)
Step 2: CROSS OUT (Reread the details. Cross out any that you decide not to include.)
Step 3: CONNECT (Connect any details that could go into one sentence.)
Step 4: NUMBER (Number the details in a logical order.)
Step 5: WRITE (Write your summary.)
Step 6: EDIT (Revise and proofread your summary.)

Prompt: Write a summary of the information you read in the *Easter Island* article.

Planning Box
(topic)
(detail)
(detail)
(detail)
(detail)
(detail)
(detail)
(detail)
(detail)
(detail)
(detail)
(detail)
(detail)

Directions: Write your summary on a separate piece of paper.

Rubric— Summary	Student or Partner Rating		Teacher Rating	
1. Did the author state the topic and the main idea in the first sentence?	Yes	Fix up	Yes	No
2. Did the author focus on important details?	Yes	Fix up	Yes	No
3. Did the author combine details in some of the sentences?	Yes	Fix up	Yes	No
4. Is the summary easy to understand?	Yes	Fix up	Yes	No
5. Did the author correctly spell words, particularly the words found in the article?	Yes	Fix up	Yes	No
6. Did the author use correct capitalization, capitalizing the first word in the sentence and proper names of people, places, and things?	Yes	Fix up	Yes	No
7. Did the author use correct punctuation, including a period at the end of each sentence?	Yes	Fix up	Yes	No

WRITING **7**

Points

(ACTIVITY A) *Vocabulary*

List 1: Tell

1.	**Egypt**	*n.* ►	(a country in northeastern Africa)
2.	**Cairo**	*n.* ►	(a city in Egypt)
3.	**Giza**	*n.* ►	(a place near Cairo)
4.	**Khufu**	*n.* ►	(a ruler of ancient Egypt)
5.	**Babylon**	*n.* ►	(an ancient city in the Middle East)
6.	**Nebuchadnezzar**	*n.* ►	(a ruler of Babylon)
7.	**Euphrates River**	*n.* ►	(a river near Babylon)
8.	**Zeus**	*n.* ►	(a Greek god)
9.	**Phideas**	*n.* ►	(a Greek sculptor)
10.	**Ephesus**	*n.* ►	(an ancient city in Turkey)
11.	**Mausolus**	*n.* ►	(an ancient king)
12.	**Halicarnassus**	*n.* ►	(an ancient city in Turkey)
13.	**Aegean Sea**	*n.* ►	(a sea between Greece and Turkey)
14.	**Helios**	*n.* ►	(the Greek sun god)
15.	**Auguste Bartholdi**	*n.* ►	(a French sculptor)
16.	**Alexandria**	*n.* ►	(a city in northern Egypt)

List 2: Strategy Practice

1.	**monument**	*n.* ►	(something [often a statue] set up to keep alive the memory of a person or event)
2.	**tribute**	*n.* ►	(something done as a sign of respect)
3.	**pyramid**	*n.* ►	(a stone structure with a square base and four sides that come up to a peak)
4.	**approximately**	*adv.* ►	(nearly)
5.	**complicate**	*v.* ►	(to make difficult or hard to understand)
6.	**commission**	*v.* ►	(to pay for work to be done)
7.	**foundation**	*n.* ►	(the base or bottom)
8.	**practical**	*adj.* ►	(showing good sense)
9.	**Colossus**	*n.* ►	(a statue of Helios, the sun god)
10.	**description**	*n.* ►	(a statement of how something looks)

TALLY ☐   VOCABULARY ◻️ **5**
Points

List 3: Word Families

Family 1	**history**	*n.*	▶ (a record of the past)
	historical	*adj.*	
	historian	*n.*	

Family 2	**architecture**	*n.*	▶ (the design, plan, and construction of buildings or other structures)
	architectural	*adj.*	
	architect	*n.*	

Family 3	**compile**	*v.*	▶ (to collect and put together)
	compiler	*n.*	
	compilation	*n.*	

Family 4	**construct**	*v.*	▶ (to make or build)
	construction	*n.*	
	deconstruct	*v.*	

Family 5	**sculpture**	*n.*	▶ (art figures and forms made of wood, stone, or clay)
	sculpt	*v.*	
	sculptor	*n.*	

ACTIVITY B *Spelling Dictation*

1.	4.
2.	5.
3.	6.

SPELLING 6
Points

(ACTIVITY C) *Background Knowledge*

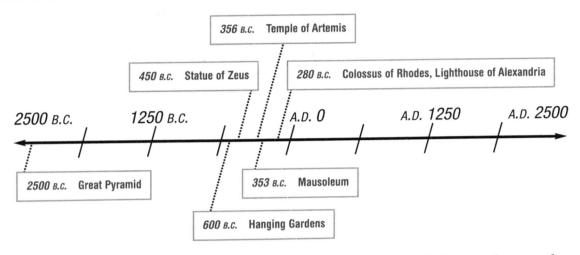

356 B.C. Temple of Artemis

450 B.C. Statue of Zeus

280 B.C. Colossus of Rhodes, Lighthouse of Alexandria

2500 B.C.   1250 B.C.   A.D. 0   A.D. 1250   A.D. 2500

2500 B.C. Great Pyramid

353 B.C. Mausoleum

600 B.C. Hanging Gardens

Everyone makes lists: lists of things to do, to buy, and to wish for. In this article, you will read about a famous list compiled by an ancient Greek writer around the second century B.C. You've probably heard of his list. It's called the Seven Wonders of the Ancient World. This list named the greatest sculptural and architectural monuments of ancient time and became one of the best-known lists of all time. The writer chose the number 7 because it was thought to be a magical number. Many other "Seven Wonders" lists have been written since then; however, the original list is the most widely accepted among historians and scholars throughout time.

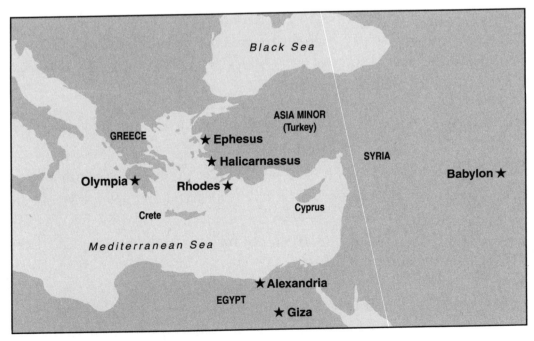

Black Sea

GREECE

ASIA MINOR
(Turkey)

★ Ephesus

★ Halicarnassus

SYRIA

Olympia ★   Rhodes ★

Babylon ★

Crete

Cyprus

Mediterranean Sea

★ Alexandria

EGYPT

★ Giza

The Locations of the Seven Wonders of the Ancient World

(ACTIVITY D) *Passage Reading and Comprehension*

The Seven Wonders of the Ancient World

As far back as the fifth century B.C., seven great monuments and structures

13 | were recognized as the Seven Wonders of the Ancient World. In the second

26 | century B.C., a Greek writer compiled the list. The buildings and monuments

38 | were tributes to science, religion, art, and power. (#1)

46 | Although only one of the Seven Wonders of the Ancient World remains

58 | intact today, historical descriptions have provided information about the others.

68 | Many of these great works inspired later architects and artists. Pieces of some of

82 | the structures, or art that they contained, can be seen at museums all around the

97 | world. (#2)

98 | **The Great Pyramid**

101 | The oldest of the Seven Wonders is also the only one that still stands today.

116 | The Great Pyramid was built in Giza (near present-day Cairo) around 2500 B.C.

130 | as a tomb for the Egyptian pharaoh Khufu. Approximately two million stones

142 | were used to build the pyramid, each weighing about two tons. The structure is

156 | so well built that you cannot even slip a card between the stones. (#3)

169 | **The Hanging Gardens of Babylon**

174 | King Nebuchadnezzar built an elaborate garden for his queen around 600

185 | B.C. Many terraced steps were constructed and then filled with plants. A

197 | complicated system of tunnels and pulleys brought water to the 300-foot-high

210 | gardens from the nearby Euphrates River. (#4)

216 | **The Statue of Zeus**

220 | In Olympia, Greece, the birthplace of the ancient Olympic games, people

231 | gathered to compete in sports and honor Zeus, an important Greek god. In the

245 | fifth century B.C., a sculptor named Phideas carved an enormous gold and ivory

258 | figure of the god. Historians believe the statue may have been 40 feet high. No

273 | trace of the statue remains today, except for reproductions (copies) that the

285 | Greeks put on their coins. (#5)

290 | **The Temple of Artemis at Ephesus**

296 | This beautiful work of architecture was built in present-day Turkey around

308 | 356 B.C. to honor the goddess Diana. It sported more than 100 columns that

322	supported a massive roof. The temple was thought to be the first structure made
336	entirely of marble. The temple was destroyed in A.D. 262 by Goths who invaded
350	the country. (#6)

352	**The Mausoleum at Halicarnassus**
356	Built in 353 B.C., the Mausoleum of Halicarnassus was a huge tomb. King
369	Mausolus commissioned the work to be built in Bodrum, a city on the Aegean Sea
384	in southwest Turkey. The massive structure and its stunning sculpture and artwork
396	remained intact for 16 centuries until it was damaged in an earthquake. Later,
409	Crusade soldiers deconstructed, or took apart, the mausoleum and used its
420	polished stone in the construction of their castle. The castle remains standing
432	today, but nothing remains at the site of the mausoleum except its foundation. (#7)

445	**The Colossus of Rhodes**
449	The Colossus was a 30-meter-tall statue of the Greek sun god, Helios. The
464	statue, which was made of bronze, was erected to guard the entrance at the
478	harbor of Rhodes, an island in Greece. It took 12 years to build and was
493	destroyed by an earthquake a mere 56 years later. It completely disappeared after
506	the pieces were sold to a man from Syria. But the wonder of the statue inspired
522	the French sculptor Auguste Bartholdi to create the Statue of Liberty. (#8)

533	**The Lighthouse of Alexandria**
537	Of the Seven Wonders, only the Lighthouse of Alexandria had a practical
549	purpose. The lighthouse helped sailors gain safe entry to the Great Harbor,
561	which is where the Nile River flows into the Mediterranean Sea. It was the
575	tallest building in the world at the time of its construction, around 280 B.C. At
590	the top was a mirror, used to reflect light from the sun or from a fire out to the
609	sea to guide sailors. Scientists are fascinated by descriptions of this mirror, which
622	was said to reflect light as far away as 35 miles. The lighthouse was weakened
637	and later destroyed by several earthquakes. (#9)
643	

(ACTIVITY E) *Fluency Building*

Cold Timing	
Practice 2	

Practice 1	
Hot Timing	

ACTIVITY F *Comprehension Questions—*
Multiple Choice and Short Answer

Comprehension Strategy—Multiple Choice

Step 1: Read the item.
Step 2: Read all of the choices.
Step 3: Think about why each choice might be correct or incorrect. Check the article as needed.
Step 4: From the possible correct choices, select the best answer.

1. (Vocabulary) **Read this sentence from the passage: "In the second century B.C., a Greek writer *compiled* the list." What does the word *compiled* mean in that sentence?**
   a. Put together items for the list.
   c. Made a pile of items for the list.
   b. Used the Greek language.
   d. Stacked up cards with names of items written on them.

2. (Cause and Effect) **The writer's purpose in creating the list of the Seven Wonders of the Ancient World was to:**
   a. have each site named a historical place.
   b. direct people to great vacation destinations.
   c. recognize very important buildings and monuments of ancient times.
   d. establish the basis for a movie on ancient accomplishments.

3. (Compare and Contrast) **How is the Great Pyramid different from the other six Wonders of the Ancient World?**
   a. The Great Pyramid is the only Wonder of the Ancient World that is a structure rather than artwork.
   b. The Great Pyramid is the only Wonder of the Ancient World that is located in Egypt.
   c. The Great Pyramid is the only Wonder of the Ancient World made from stone.
   d. The Great Pyramid is the only Wonder of the Ancient World that still stands today.

4. (Main Idea) **Which sentence gives the best summary of the article?**
   a. The "Seven Wonders of the Ancient World" list names monuments that all educated people should visit.
   b. The "Seven Wonders of the Ancient World" list contains important buildings and monuments of ancient times.
   c. The Seven Wonders of the Ancient World were so important that no current structure or monument will ever be greater.
   d. The Greek writer compiled the list for his own use in planning vacations.

MULTIPLE CHOICE COMPREHENSION

4

Points

Comprehension Strategy—Short Answer

Step 1: Read the item.

Step 2: Turn the question into part of the answer and write it down.

Step 3: Think of the answer or locate the answer in the article.

Step 4: Complete your answer.

1. How did we learn about these ancient wonders?

_____

_____

_____

_____

_____

2. Why do you think these seven things were chosen to be the Seven Wonders of the Ancient World?

_____

_____

_____

_____

_____

SHORT ANSWER COMPREHENSION

Points

(ACTIVITY G) *Expository Writing—Extended Response*

Writing Strategy—Extended Response

Step 1: LIST (List the reasons for your position. For each reason, explain with details.)

Step 2: CROSS OUT (Reread your reasons and details. Cross out any that you decide not to include.)

Step 3: CONNECT (Connect any details that could go into one sentence.)

Step 4: NUMBER (Number the reasons in a logical order.)

Step 5: WRITE (Write your response.)

Step 6: EDIT (Revise and proofread your response.)

Prompt: What three modern inventions do you think have made the most difference in the world and why?

Planning Box
(position)
(reason)
(explain)
(reason)
(explain)
(reason)
(explain)

Directions: Write your extended response on a separate piece of paper.

Rubric— Extended Response	Student or Partner Rating		Teacher Rating	
1. Did the author tell his/her position in the first sentence?	Yes	Fix up	Yes	No
2. Did the author include at least three **strong, logical** reasons for his/her position?	Yes	Fix up	Yes	No
3. Did the author provide a **strong, logical** explanation for each of his/her reasons?	Yes	Fix up	Yes	No
4. Is the response easy to understand?	Yes	Fix up	Yes	No
5. Did the author correctly spell words, particularly the words found in the article?	Yes	Fix up	Yes	No
6. Did the author use correct capitalization, capitalizing the first word in the sentence and proper names of people, places, and things?	Yes	Fix up	Yes	No
7. Did the author use correct punctuation, including a period at the end of each sentence?	Yes	Fix up	Yes	No

WRITING   **7**
Points

REWARDS Strategies for Reading Long Words

Overt Strategy

1. Circle the prefixes.

2. Circle the suffixes.

3. Underline the vowels.

4. Say the parts of the word.

5. Say the whole word.

6. Make it a real word.

   Example:

   (re)(con)struc(tion)

Covert Strategy

1. Look for prefixes, suffixes, and vowels.

2. Say the parts of the word.

3. Say the whole word.

4. Make it a real word.

Prefixes, Suffixes, and Vowel Combinations Reference Chart

	Decoding Element	Key Word	Decoding Element	Key Word	Decoding Element	Key Word
Prefixes	a	above	com	compare	mis	mistaken
	ab	abdomen	con	continue	multi	multiage
	ac	accommodate	de	depart	over	overpopulate
	ad	advertise	dis	discover	per	permit
	af	afford	en	entail	pre	prevent
	ap	appreciate	ex	example	pro	protect
	ar	arrange	hydro	hydrothermal	re	return
	as	associate	im	immediate	sub	submarine
	at	attention	in	insert	trans	translate
	auto	automatic	ir	irregular	un	uncover
	be	belong	micro	microscope		
Suffixes	able	disposable	ful	careful	ness	kindness
	age	courage	ible	reversible	or	tailor
	al	final	ic	frantic	ous	nervous
	ance	disturbance	ing	running	s	birds
	ant	dormant	ion	million	ship	ownership
	ate	regulate	ish	selfish	sion	mission
	ary	military	ism	realism	sive	expensive
	cial	special	ist	artist	tial	partial
	cious	precious	ity	oddity	tive	attentive
	ed	landed	ize	criticize	tion	action
	ence	essence	le	cradle	tious	cautious
	ent	consistent	less	useless	ture	picture
	er	farmer	ly	safely	y	industry
	est	biggest	ment	argument		
Vowel Combinations	ai	rain	ou	loud	a–e	make
	au	sauce	ow	low, down	e–e	Pete
	ay	say	oy	boy	i–e	side
	ee	deep	ar	farm	o–e	hope
	ea	meat, thread	er	her	u–e	use
	oa	foam	ir	bird		
	oi	void	or	torn		
	oo	moon, book	ur	turn		

Review Lessons Chart

Name _____   Teacher _____

	Activities A–C (4 possible Participation Points)	Activities D and E (4 possible Participation Points)	Activity F Reading Check (4 possible Performance Points)	SUBTOTAL POINTS (12 possible points)	BONUS POINTS	TOTAL POINTS	LESSON GRADE
Review Lesson 1							
Review Lesson 2							
Review Lesson 3							
Review Lesson 4							
Review Lesson 5							
Review Lesson 6							

Participation Points (Possible Points: 4)

- Following behavioral guidelines
- Paying attention
- Participating
- Responding accurately

Performance Points (Possible Points: 4)

No errors	**4 points**
1 error	**3 points**
2 errors	**2 points**
More than 2 errors	**0 points**

Application Lessons Chart

Name _____   Teacher _____

	Activity A List 1 and List 2 (4 possible Participation Points)	Oral Vocabulary Tally (5 possible Performance Points)	Activity A List 3 (4 possible Participation Points)	Activity B Spelling (6 possible Performance Points)	Activity D Passage Reading (4 possible Participation Points)	Activity E Fluency (4 possible Performance Points)	Activity F Multiple Choice (4 possible Performance Points)	Activity F Short Answer (4 possible Performance Points)	Activity G Writing (7 possible Performance Points)	SUBTOTAL POINTS (42 possible points)	BONUS POINTS	TOTAL POINTS	LESSON GRADE
Application Lesson 1								4					
Application Lesson 2								4					
Application Lesson 3								4					
Application Lesson 4													
Application Lesson 5													
Application Lesson 6													
Application Lesson 7													
Application Lesson 8													
Application Lesson 9													
Application Lesson 10													
Application Lesson 11													
Application Lesson 12													
Application Lesson 13													
Application Lesson 14													
Application Lesson 15													

Fluency Graph

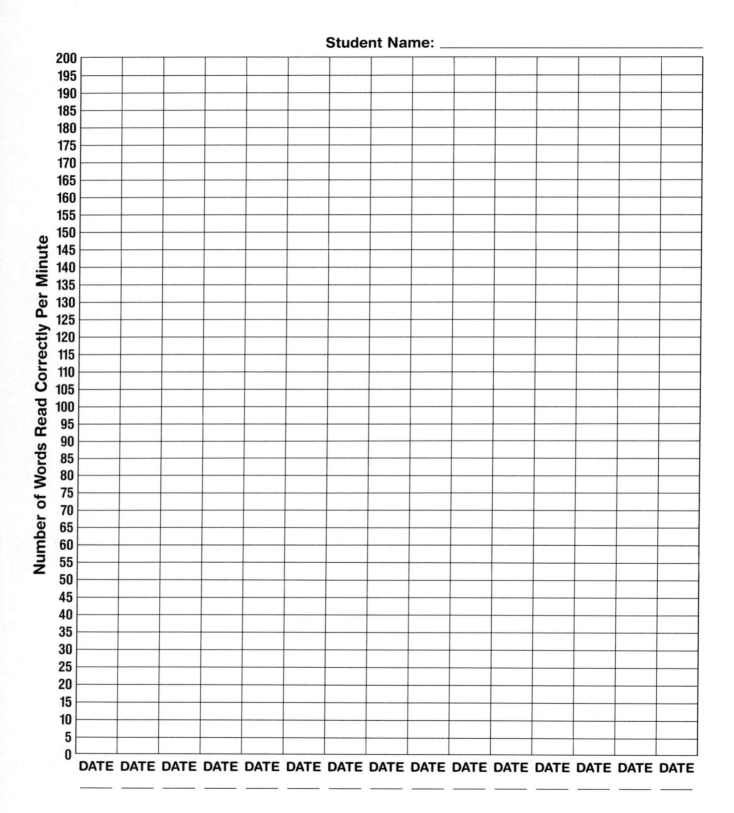

Student Name: _____

Number of Words Read Correctly Per Minute

200
195
190
185
180
175
170
165
160
155
150
145
140
135
130
125
120
115
110
105
100
95
90
85
80
75
70
65
60
55
50
45
40
35
30
25
20
15
10
5
0

DATE   DATE   DATE   DATE   DATE   DATE   DATE   DATE   DATE   DATE   DATE   DATE   DATE   DATE   DATE